THE MESSAGE IN THE MIRACLES OF CHRIST

Releasing God's Power into the Church Today

Donna Carlisle

Lighthouse Publications

The Message in the Miracles of Christ
by Donna Carlisle

Printed in the United States of America
ISBN 0-9642211-3-6

Unless otherwise indicated, Bible quotations are taken from the New International Version.

Designer
Scott Wallis & Associates
1100 Larkin Ave.
Northwest Suite
Elgin, IL 60123
(847) 468-1457
www.scottwallis.org

Publisher
Lighthouse Publications
1100 Larkin Ave.
Northwest Suite
Elgin, IL 60123
(847) 697-6788

Author
Donna Carlisle
222 McKinley Avenue
Geneva, IL 50134
(630) 845-8154

<u>Acknowledgements</u>

Pastor Sandy Schoeber – My mentor, friend and example in walking with my Lord and the one who encouraged me to write these revelations down.

Gene – My husband and friend – with many thanks for your patience, encouragement and wisdom in helping to guide me.

Foreword

This book is full of end time revelation! It is a must read for every Christian leader, or anyone who hungers for the deep things of God. It will inspire you to look closer at the Word of God for true revelations from heaven.

We know that in the Bible there are wonderful hidden mysteries. Paul wrote in 1 Corinthians 4:1,2, "Let a man so consider us, as servants of Christ and stewards of the mysteries of God. Moreover it is required in stewards that one be found faithful."

As Donna, a faithful steward of the Lord, sought Him in the Word, in prayer and in worship, He began to reveal to her the depth of His miracles that were recorded for us to study. As you read the following pages, you will begin to have a divine understanding as to why these particular miracles were recorded. There were countless other miracles that Jesus performed, but the Father wanted to share these with His people. The Bible tells us that had all the works of Jesus been recorded, the world could not contain the books necessary to record them all. You will see that there is a prophetic message to each of these miracles.

Donna wrote this book after knowing true intimacy with her Master. As she poured her oil out through worship at His feet, He took her through His miracles. As you read this book, let Him take you through each miracle and be transformed by the knowledge fo the deep truth that will be revealed to you. These spiritual truths will take you to another level in knowing our Lord.

My husband and I have had the privilege of pastoring Donna and have been blessed to call her our dear friend. With complete confidence we urge you to take this book and study it with all your heart. Donna walks with God and she hears His voice. You will want to read and study this exciting adventure through the miracles of Jesus. I highly recommend it to you! Be blessed as you read.

Pastor Sandy Schoeber
Greater Glory Family Worship
Glen Carbon, Illinois

Introduction

In an open vision on day, I found myself riding a horse beside my Lord. We were in a company of soldiers, dusty and battle weary but elated. There were people lined up on both sides of the road shouting and cheering. Ahead, not too far in the distance, was an ancient wall with an open gate, which was our destination. Lined up on top of the wall were more people, rejoicing.

The thing I remember most about this vision was not what I saw, but what I felt. There was a complete unity among every person on horseback. We had been through the battle and won. Moreover, I knew each person would have given their life for me, as I would joyfully give mine for them. We rode together in complete peace, harmony and joy.

Jesus leaned over to me, and I reached for His hand and leaned toward him, turning my ear to hear through noise of the crowd as He said, "We did it!" I laughed jubilantly, and awoke.

This vision speaks of the unity God wants for His body, His church. One in thought and purpose to bring the kingdom of God to earth. We are soldiers in a battle for the souls of the harvest. In this battle, we will trample the serpent and tread upon the lion that roars against us.

To accomplish this, we must understand what Christ bought fo rus on the cross. Salvation, yes, but in the original greek the word for salvation also means healing, deliverance and abundance. As we grasp what God did for us, we will complete the restoration Jesus began. He is the first born of the dead, we have died with Him and we live in Him. He wants us to have everything He purchased for us through His death.

Unity is essential to be part of the army of God. He has not divided us, but united us through the cross. Every believer is my brother or sister. I am one with them as I am one with Christ. Through God's love, we can learn to love as He does. Love each other and love each one Christ died for. This means every single person on the planet.

The picture God paints for us in the miracles show us how Jesus longs to move through each one of us today. He wants us all to walk in signs and wonders as He did. The false teachings regarding miracles within much of the church has historically paralyzed believers with unbelief. We must move beyond this, reach up and begin accomplishing all that Jesus said we could do. We can do this by taking a fresh look at God's word and realize He really did mean what He said. Every word of God is true. He has not changed His mind one bit about what He said. You and I can do what Jesus said we can do.

Contents

Chapter One

• The Message in the Miracles of Christ •

The Miracles were Prophetic

In my kitchen, baking bread and praying in tongues, I heard God's voice inside of me say, "The miracles were prophetic."

Baking bread is a joy for me. Granted, I make a mess. My son-in-law Glenn says there's flour blowing off the ceiling fan, but it's fun to smell the warm yeast and press the soft dough through my hands. It gives me a chance to pray, and I usually pray in tongues. One day last week, while elbow deep in sticky-goo and covered with flour, I heard God's voice inside of me say, "The miracles were prophetic."

Startled, I said, "What Lord? What does that mean?"

He told me to look at the wedding in Cana, and then outlined an interpretation of the prophecy. I was astounded as I got my Bible and read it, finding information that spoke to the Church.

We were preparing to go to Chicago for a visit with our children, so I sort of shelved the whole idea with the thought that I would check out the other miracles later. We came home on Saturday, tired after a busy trip, and on Sunday God brought two other miracles to my mind.

I became more and more amazed as I prayed over them, and God revealed the same type of information. After sharing these revelations with my pastor, she encouraged me to write them down.

The next morning during my Bible study, God told me to read the eighth chapter of Matthew, and revelation poured out with every miracle listed. At that time, the quiet voice of God told me this was a message for the End-Time Church.

With tears streaming down my face, I called my pastor and read the notes I had written in my journal to her. She was in agreement that the material was scriptural, and suggested I continue to study and record it.

This is simply a message from God through me to His Church, and I want to assure you I do not believe it is in any way authoritative or equal with Scripture. It is an interpretation of Scripture, filtered through my heart, mind and belief system.

This is also in no way a suggestion that these miracles did not really happen. I want to be very clear that I believe the Word of God to be true, and everything that is stated in Scripture really happened historically. I believe there are often messages within messages, and the Bible can be read on many levels. The advice God gave Abraham or David can still be applied to my life. The children of Israel came out of Egypt and actually trekked those long hard miles to the Promised Land, but I can also use their trip as an analogy and "type" to benefit my walk with God.

I have no idea why God chose to share this with a housewife in a little town outside of St. Louis. You just have to wonder sometimes at His sense of humor. I figure I will write the message, and it is

His job to get it out. I want to assure you I have no formal Bible training, was not born in a Christian family, never finished college, have absolutely no qualifications for this project, and writing is not my favorite past-time.

God led me to the 10th chapter of John for scripture today, and I was amazed to read in the 25th verse, "The miracles I do in My Father's Name speak for me," and "Believe the miracles that you may learn and understand," in the 30th verse. This was an undeniable message from God so it is in obedience to his voice I will attempt to write His message to the Last Days Church. I feel I am on an incredible journey with Him, and I am so glad you have joined us.

The First Miracle

The miracle at the wedding in Cana is recorded only in John 2:1-11.

On the third day, a wedding took place at Cana in Galilee.

This first miracle of Jesus was performed at Cana at a wedding. The first event of the Kingdom is already scheduled; it will be a wedding. We read in Revelation 19:7:

Hallelujah! For our Lord God Almighty reigns. Let us rejoice and be glad and give Him glory! For the wedding of the Lamb has come and His Bride has made herself ready. Fine linen, bright and clean, was given her to wear.

The wedding of Revelation takes place in John's vision of heaven right after the fall of Babylon, and before Jesus rides out on a white horse with the armies of heaven following Him. It will be the glorious wedding banquet God has prepared for all of His believers.

The name of the town "Cana" comes from "Canaan" which is the name of the Promised Land before the Israelites conquered it. We are supposed to be battling the forces of evil, evicting them and then living in the land of the promises. The Church has been asleep to the promises, but she will wake up and grasp them for the first time since she lost her power centuries ago.

The wedding in Cana happened on the third day, and Scriptures state, "A day of the Lord is as a thousand years." Since two thousand years have passed since the beginning of the Church, the wedding supper of the Lamb has to take place on the third day.

There is a passage of Scripture in Hosea 6:2 that reads in the King James version, "After two days He will revive us: in the third day He will raise us up, and we shall live in His sight."

This is the final flash of glory for the Church, which will lead into the darkness of the Tribulation. The last rays of the power of God on this earth will shine with a brightness never seen before. Then the Tribulation, which is the darkest night the world shall ever know, will begin. After that, the Son shall come to earth and there will be no more night. The day of the millennium will dawn.

Jesus' mother was there, and Jesus and his disciples had also been invited to the wedding.

All of the disciples were invited to this wedding, and of course all of His Church is invited to the wedding of Jesus and His Bride. It wouldn't be much of a wedding without part of the Bride!

When the Wine was Gone

The state of the Church for the last 1800 years has been dry. There has been little wine of the Holy Spirit in a Body deprived of the Word for hundreds of years, and then divided by denominational in-

8

fighting. The Church has been in desperate need of wine, and wine in the Bible is an analogy for the Holy Spirit. Most of the Church has denied the presence and power of the Holy Spirit in the lives of the believer.

Jesus' mother said to him, "They have no more wine."

Moms always know what to do in a crisis. When our wine is gone, we have no place to go but to Jesus. When the Church comes to Him with a need, He is there to fill it.

Dear woman, why do you involve Me? Jesus replied. "My time has not yet come."

His ministry had begun, He had chosen His disciples and He had been baptized and anointed with the Spirit. Why did He say "His time had not come"? Because it was not yet time for *His* wedding, which is 2,000 years into the future. That will be His day, His time, and I believe that day is soon at hand.

His mother said to the servants, "Do whatever He tells you."

Here is the advice that would get the Church back on track. Its about time God's people listened to His voice and His word and do whatever He tells them. The only way to accomplish the work God has for the End-Time Church is obedience. Abandon the programs and the schedules and fall in love with the Groom. No marriage is going to make it without a loving and obedient Bride.

Nearby stood six stone water jars, the kind used by the Jews for ceremonial washing, each holding from twenty to thirty gallons.

The number six in the Bible is the number for man. The vessels were there, clean and ready. We are not ready for the water or the wine until we are holy and have washed our vessels through true repentance. Then we will be a group of people cleansed and waiting for a move of God.

The number twenty in Hebrew means "the power to suppress or lift up." The Church has the power to suppress the powers of darkness and lift up mankind through Christ. The number thirty means "to learn, to teach." The Church must learn of God and then go out and teach others. Jesus began His ministry when He was thirty. It is time we were of age, and began to teach the fullness of the Gospel He gave us.

Jesus said to the servants, "Fill the jars with water;" so they filled them to the brim.

Jesus commanded His servants by His Word to fill the jars with water and they filled them to the brim. No half-full or partially full jars for them! The Church must be filled to the brim with the Spirit, by obedience to the Word, before the new wine will come. The Spirit is the water and through the Word, within the vessel, it becomes the wine.

Then He told them, "Now draw some out and take it to the master of the banquet."

The new wine is then taken to the master of the banquet. It is when the Church goes back to Jesus, becomes obedient to what He says, and is filled with the Spirit that we as a Body are prepared to come before the Father. It is to restore us to the Father that Jesus came. We take our wine to Him in worship and praise and thanksgiving, with great joy entering His presence. It is a time of celebration!!

They did so, and the master of the banquet tasted the water that had been turned into wine. He did not realize where it had come from, though the servants knew. Then he called the Bridegroom aside and said, "Everyone brings out the choice wine first and then the cheaper wine after the guests

11

have had too much to drink; but you have saved the best till now."

The wine of our worship has now been presented to our Father God, and He declares it is better than the old! The Last Day Church will be far more powerful and impact the world in a greater way than the Church of Acts and the New Testament. He is coming for His glorious Bride, without spot or wrinkle.

This, the first of His miraculous signs, Jesus performed at Cana in Galilee. He thus revealed His glory, and His disciples put their faith in Him.

Through this Church, working with miraculous signs, God is going to reveal the glory of Jesus Christ to the world. As His present day disciples put their faith in a living Savior, filled with power and wonder, the greatest mission that has ever come to earth will be completed with victory! Many half hearted, luke-warm Christians will come to Him when they behold His Glory, revealed to them by the power of the Last Day Church.

A wedding is a time of celebration. This End-Time Church will be filled with joy. It is a time for great jubilation in the Body of Christ. The laughter of the Holy Spirit has been one of the first signs of the movement of God in this day. The Spirit has blessed me with dance in my worship times. My husband, Gene, says this is a true creative miracle, for I had absolutely no rhythm. When people would clap I would have to watch someone to stay on beat. But now, in the Spirit, I dance with abandon, keeping perfect time to the music. We will see an increase in the laughter and the dance, in the full expression of our joy in the Lord.

Sometimes, when I dance, I invite Jesus to come and dance with me. His presence is so awesome and real during those times. He is longing for a personal intimate relationship with each one of us. A knowing as deep and personal as that between a Bride and groom. There is great joy as we become one with Him.

Fill the Nets

The miracle of a large catch of fish after an entire night of fishing is in the Bible twice. The first time is when Jesus called His disciples Peter, James, John and Andrew, written in Luke 5:1-11. This is written for the Church of Acts and has the same interpretation for that Church as the second miracle does for the Last Days Church.

13

We will look at the second miracle of the fish from John 21:1-14.

Afterward Jesus appeared again to His disciples by the Sea of Tiberias.

It is time for Jesus to appear again for those who follow Him. There is a new call to the Church, a new dispensation about to fall from our Father's hand. Oddly enough, the Sea of Galilee is called the Sea of Tiberias in this passage. This is the Roman name for it taken from the third emperor of Rome, Tiberius Claudius Nero. The Church that Jesus is appearing to this time is basically a Gentile Church.

It happened this way: Simon Peter, Thomas (called Didymus), Nathanael from Cana in Galilee, the sons of Zebedee, and two other disciples were together.

Seven of the disciples were there, and seven is the number of perfection in the Scriptures. Simon Peter was the leader. Thomas' last name Didymus means "a twin." This stands for the two Churches that are anointed with power; the Church of Acts and the Last Days Church.

Nathaniel, who was referred to by Jesus as a "*true Israelite, in whom there is nothing false*" in John 2:48, came from Galilee which means circle.

The circle of the Church has come again, and it will be a true Church, in the same power and might as the Church of the New Testament. All that is false in this Church will be eliminated.

John and James are there, and Zebedee, their Father's name, means Jehovah's gift. From the very hand of Jehovah will pour out gifts and miracles on the Last Days Church.

"I'm going out to fish," Simon Peter told them, and they said, "We'll go with you."

The leaders of the early Church went out to fish. The results of that first fishing expedition I have already referred to is the miracle recorded in Luke. Their nets were so full they began to break, and the two boats began to sink. The two boats are the Jewish Church and the Gentile Church, and the catch was so large the boats couldn't hold it. The Church lost their first love and sank over the years. The nets broke and the vessels were crippled as the power hungry and self-seeking leaders quenched the true power of God. The flame died.

So they went out and got in the boat, but that night they caught nothing.

For two thousand years, the Church has had "slim pickin's." It has been wildly successful in the eyes of the world, gaining money and prestige. The true mission of the Church however, to restore each of us to our Father God, has failed. We have great social programs and entertaining Sunday services, with pomp and ceremony, but the heart is dead. The great commission that Christ entrusted to His people has never been realized through the long dark night.

Early in the morning, Jesus stood on the shore, but the disciples did not realize that it was Jesus.

The sun is coming up, and the dawn is breaking. This is a new day for the Church. He has stood up and is on the shore, and His disciples do not recognize Him. The Church has been satisfied with religiosity. She does not know her Lord when He comes.

He called out to them, "Friends, do you have any fish?"

Christ is calling out to His people, asking how full their nets are. Most churches are not gaining members; they are losing them. Children of strong Christian families have wandered away. The fire burning within the Church has not blazed consistently since the Church of Acts.

"No," they answered.

I'm afraid if we are honest, the nets are empty. Even the new converts we get in are difficult to keep.

He said, "Throw your net on the right side of the boat, and you will find some."

We have been fishing on the wrong side of the boat! We have looked at every solution but God's. The Spirit filled committed Christians can turn this world upside down as they did in the days of Acts. We can do it faster and better for we have a great communication system and amazing resources available to us. But we must turn to God with our whole heart, mind and soul and each of us must develop a personal relationship with our heavenly Father through Jesus Christ and by the Holy Spirit.

When they did, they were unable to haul the net in because of the large number of fish.

The harvest for the Last Days Church is going to be so large it will stun the world. People will be jumping into the nets, and they will overflow with new believers. The Church needs to prepare for this harvest.

*Then the disciple whom Jesus loved said,
"It is the Lord!"*

Jesus loves us, and those that love Him will have their eyes opened and the Church will recognize their Lord.

As soon as Simon Peter heard him say, "It is the Lord," he wrapped his outer garment around him (for he had taken it off) and jumped into the water.

The leaders have removed their garment, their anointed covering, and they shall put it back on. They will then jump into the water – talk about revival! The leaders will leap over the sides of the boat and swim to their Lord.

The other disciples followed in the boat, towing the net full of fish, for they were not far from shore, about a hundred yards.

The faithful followers of Christ bring in the catch, taking care to prevent loss of even one. The time is near at hand, for the boat is not far from shore. This translation says 100 yards, but that is 200 cubits in the Greek, and the Church renewal started about 200 years ago. We are very close to the end.

When they landed, they saw a fire of burning coals there with fish on it, and some bread.

The fish must, of course, be dead to be of any use. We must die to ourselves to live to Him. After the water came the fire. The fish were laying on burning coals representing the fire of the Holy Spirit. The bread is the Bread of Heaven, Jesus.

Jesus said to them, "Bring some of the fish you just caught."

When we have a new believer, we have to learn to lead him into a relationship with the risen Lord. They must be filled with the Spirit and put through the fire before they will be of use to the Kingdom. Discipleship is crucial to prevent the loss of the catch. Without the fire they will rot.

When our son, Scott, was about 3 years old he caught his first fish, which was about 4 inches long. He carried it everywhere he went, and took it home with us. The next day, there was this strange odor in the house; that fish had begun to rot. We need to take a good long sniff to see what kind of fragrance we are giving off. Is it the aroma of the Holy Spirit or the smell of a dead fish that has not been through the fire?

Simon Peter climbed aboard and dragged the net ashore. It was full of large fish, 153, but even with so many the net was not torn.

The leaders will jump in and take a dip in the waters, then go through the fire, but they must then be sure to help the followers to do the same. Peter went back to the boat and made sure the catch made it to shore. This time there was only one boat and it did not sink nor was the net torn.

Denominational lines must fall and all need to realize we are one Body. Each denomination reveals a truth that has been recovered through the ages of the Church. Every truth is necessary, but each generation of the Church must include ALL truth. We can learn much from the historical revelations of God's truth that were revealed to establish each denominational body.

The 153 large fish represent nations that will be brought into the net before the end. It will take the assistance of every leader and every believer to haul in the enormous catch that is about to come in.

There is far too much division in the Body of Christ over doctrinal issues. A person can become a carpenter and build a house with a hammer and a hand saw. He can use a string with a nail for a plumb line and a tin can for a level. As long as he has the knowledge of how to build and to use the tools he owns, he can build a house with them. But, if he really wants to build a house quickly and efficiently, he'll need some power tools.

My husband Gene loves Norm Abram on PBS, and drools over his workshop full of tools. The Church needs the power tools to finish the assignment God has given her for this day. Just as the hand tools served many generations to build their homes, but have given way to the speed and efficiency of electrical machines, so has the Church passed the place that we can build without the power of the Spirit. Get your hands on every gift God has provided in His Word.

Jesus said to them, "Come and have breakfast."

The Lord has prepared a meal for us, and is inviting us to come and eat. It is time we turned to Him and had fellowship with Him. He is our King, and yet He is there to serve. He will feed this Church and care for its needs. Each of us needs to spend breakfast with Jesus, asking His direction for our day. Eat what He has fixed, share our lives and catch His vision.

None of the disciples dared to ask Him, "Who are you?" They knew it was the Lord.

We must *know* the Lord, and how can we know Him if we do not spend time with Him? When we commune with Him, we will have no doubts that it is His move and His plan in action. We will recognize the hand of the King. We will know His voice.

Jesus came, took the bread and gave it to them, and did the same with the fish.

He is our daily bread. He has come to feed us, and He gives us the fish to strengthen us to feed others. We grow as we are prepared and "cooked" in the Holy Spirit, ready to be used to spread His Word. There is an element in discipleship that as you voluntarily yield to Christ through your leaders, the self in you is "eaten." Until the self is consumed, Christ cannot be manifested in us. We must each lose our life to save it.

The Spirit is arising again, and the leaders are taking the disciples back out. The nets have been mended, and the vessels are newer and more modern. A technologically advanced people of God are catching the vision and have gotten back into a better boat with stronger nets. This time we shall not fail.

• The Message in the Miracles of Christ •

Chapter Two

Wealth of the World

The financial system of the Kingdom is not like that of the world. The people of God have a higher and better economy.

The miracle of the coin found in the mouth of a fish is recorded in Matthew 17:24-27.

After Jesus and His disciples arrive in Capernaum, the collectors of the two-drachma tax came to Peter and asked; "Doesn't your teacher pay the temple tax?"

27

Jesus lived in Capernaum during His ministry. This was His home and the people there rejected His ministry. He says in Luke 10:15, "And you, Capernaum, will you be lifted up to the skies? No, you will go down to the depths." They were too familiar with Him, He was their next-door neighbor, and they could not see Him as the Son of God, in spite of the miracles. They wanted the God of the temple to pay tax to Himself.

The Church has taxed the Lord, and He has allowed it to go to the depths. The church of unbelief and doubt will not be the one that is lifted to the skies. It will be those who recognize Him and accept the miraculous ministry that He is about to bring forth that shall be lifted up, as He was lifted up. Through the power of the cross comes the resurrection glory.

"Yes, He does," he replied.

It would appear that they normally paid the taxes when they were due, and Peter thought this was a legitimate expense. Peter obviously did not have any money in his pocket, so he took his need to Jesus.

When Peter came into the house Jesus was the first to speak.

28

Jesus knew what Peter wanted even before he walked in the door! Whether or not it was a legitimate tax, Jesus knew Peter thought it was. He was there to meet that need, as He is there to meet every need.

"What do you think, Simon?" He asked. "From whom do the kings of the earth collect duty and taxes - from their own sons or from others?" "From others," Peter answered. "Then the sons are exempt", Jesus said to him.

A king does not collect money from his own children, or the princes and princesses living in his palace. No, he collects taxes from the populace, and he gives great gifts to his children. The duty we owe is only to God.

We are the children of the Most High God! In this Last Day Church He will collect from the people of satan's kingdom, and they will support the Church. The wealth of the wicked has been stored up for the righteous.

"But so that we may not offend them, go to the lake and throw out your line. Take the first fish you catch; open its mouth and you will find a four-drachma coin. Take it and give it to them for My tax and yours."

He told Peter to go to the water and throw out his line. A line can be used as a metaphor for speech, and the money was in the mouth of the fish. When we open our mouth with a confession of God's promises for us financially, all of our needs will be met. Open your mouth and the "script" of God's Word will pour out gold.

The Lord did not provide the money for the other disciples who did not ask. It was not a 26-drachma coin, but a 4-drachma coin, half for Peter's need and half for Jesus. You must do your own asking and your own confession.

In Isaiah 60:5 the Scripture promises, "The wealth on the seas will be brought to you, to you the riches of the nations will come." There will be an avalanche of wealth for the final hour of the Church, and the wealth of the wicked shall come to God's anointed people. These riches are coming into our hands to meet our legitimate needs and to finance the End-Time harvest for the Church.

The financial system of the Kingdom is not like that of the world. The people of God have a higher and better economy. When using God's prosperity principles you cannot fail to have abundance.

Larry Hutton came and taught for four days at our little church, and the tithes and offerings doubled. One of our teens put 57 cents in the offering during a meeting, which was all that he had, and received $120 the next day in tips at work. He usually only gets about $20 a day as a bus boy in a local restaurant!

Wake Up, Lord!

The story of Jesus calming the storm is told in Mark 4:37-41.

That day when evening came, He said to his disciples, "Let us go over to the other side."

In Christ's first day here, the evening came, and He told His disciples He was going to the other side. He left this earth, and went to rejoin His heavenly Father.

Leaving the crowd behind, they took Him along, just as He was, in the boat.

The crowds that did not really know Him were left behind, but the disciples carried Him with them in their hearts. He is the same Jesus; they took Him just as He was. He was in the boat with them

31

in the form of the Holy Spirit. The Holy Spirit is here to reveal the real Jesus to us.

There were also other boats with Him.

The disciples and others formed a group of boats that took off in faith, headed for the other side. These represent the faithful, of many creeds and kinds, those who left the crowd and carried Him with them. The other boats were "*with HIM,*" not "with them," meaning they were true followers of Christ even though there were different names painted on the bow of each vessel. There are many denominations, but we are one in Christ.

A furious squall came up, and the waves broke over the boat, so that it was nearly swamped.

The devil is furious at the rebirth of the Spirit in the Kingdom of God here on Earth, and his squall is reaching to heaven. He is reading the last of Revelation and knows his time is short. The waves of his fury are beginning to break over the vessels of the Church, and it has been nearly swamped. Divisions and gossip and criticism have buffeted the leaders. Voices have been raised by those who feel it is their calling to point fingers and denounce the faithful. Wickedness abounds in the land and in the Church.

Jesus was in the stern, sleeping on a cushion.

The Church is in a mess and it seems as though Jesus is asleep. Curled up on a cushion He appears to be oblivious to the storm swirling about the boat. How can He not see the need, doesn't He know we are desperate for Him now?

The disciples woke Him and said, "Teacher, don't you care if we drown?"

The disciples cried to Him to "Wake up!" The teacher, Jesus, was needed to rescue them. The Church today feels like it is drowning in its battle with the world forces. Jesus has come to teach us again through His miracles. This is a Last Day message to His Church to prepare for Him, for He has stood up and they must be ready.

He got up, rebuked the wind and said to the waves, "Quiet, be still"

The confusion and terror of this day will end when we rebuke the wind and talk to the waves in His name. Quiet, be still. He has risen up within us, His Church, and He is getting ready to return for His inheritance.

Then the wind died down and it was completely calm.

There is no force in the universe that can stand against Him. When He speaks, it happens. He is coming for His Church. He is standing up, and the wind and the waves cannot exist in His presence. It is time to rise up with Him and use the authority He has imparted to us.

He asked his disciples, "Why are you so afraid? Do you still have no faith?"

He is asking us why we live in fear of the curse of the earth. The storms of life will not affect us when we boldly step out and use our faith. We have the Word on computer disks, on audiotapes, in our churches, in libraries full of books explaining and expounding upon it. There is a veritable explosion of information being poured into us through Christian television and videos. But we still have no faith.

Faith is the Word *IN* us, living and working His miracles, changing lives and powerfully affecting all with whom we come in contact. There is an excitement and passion that accompanies true faith, and will Christ find it on earth when He returns?

*They were terrified and asked each other,
"Who is this? Even the winds and the
waves obey Him."*

There is an element of fear when we meet the
real Jesus; the One filled with power and might. I
recently had a vision of Him as King of Kings and
Lord of Lords, and I will never be the same. There
may be terror in the Church when Christ begins to
do the Signs and Wonders in this last age. Many do
not know that Jesus. They are used to the pretty
Jesus in their stained glass windows – a
comfortable Jesus who doesn't get too close, and is
not a true force or power. There will be many in the
coming days that will say, "Who is this?"

Either the winds and the waves obey your Jesus,
or you don't really know who He is. Make sure you
get acquainted with the true Master. He is here to
break every bond and set the captives free. You
need the powerful and authoritative ruler of the
universe. Don't accept an imitation Lord.

Even the most anointed churches and pastors
are not moving in the full power of the Spirit. They
don't walk down the street and have people lined
up hoping their shadow will fall on them. When
they go to the mall, no one gets up out of a wheel
chair by the Power that resides on them. When the

last move of God really hits, we will realize how bereft of the mighty power of God we have been. Let's get ready for the greater works He said we would do.

Multiplication Tables

The miracle of the loaves and fishes is another event that is found twice in the Scriptures. The feeding of the 5,000 is the only miracle that is in all four Gospels. The first miracle is written for the Church of Acts, just like the dual miracles of the great catch of fish. We will look at the second occurrence, which is the feeding of the 4,000, found in Mark 8:1, and has a message for the Last Days Church.

During those days, another large crowd gathered.

Wherever Jesus is, a crowd follows. In this day, as people of God begin displaying signs and wonders through their ministry, crowds will gather.

Since they had nothing to eat, Jesus called His disciples to Him and said, "I have compassion for these people; they have already been with Me three days and have nothing to eat."

The Church is hungry for the living bread. It has been centuries since it has been fed the true Word. The people have had Twinkies and sugar-coated cereals, but the living bread of Jesus and the meat of the Word has been withheld. The miracles of God can not have ended; they are the power of the Word. The Church has been guilty of having a form of Godliness, but denying its power (2 Tim 3:5).

If I send them home hungry, they will collapse on the way, because some of them have come a long distance.

The hungry people of God are ready to collapse. Jesus is the Way, and He wants to sustain His people with true nourishment. The watered down Gospel does not feed the people who have come a long way. They need the complete and vital Word of God.

We had Jim and Vicky Crick visit, and after a long trip, they came in to find me making home-made rolls. The smell of the fresh bread permeated the house when they arrived, and they hung out in the kitchen to grab some as soon as they came out of the oven. Jim and Vicky's hunger was intensified by the aroma of the freshly baked bread, just as the people of God are being turned on to God as they get a whiff of the complete power of the Full Gospel in His latest move.

The people of God need answers to the problems in their lives. The power to break addictions, heal marriages that are on the rocks, deal with rebellious children, to break the bondage of sickness and debt. They have come a long distance and need healing, nourishment and rest.

But where in this remote place can anyone get enough bread to feed them?

From where is the bread coming? They are not near a 24-hour supermarket, and there are no Golden Arches in sight. The Church is in need, but where are the resources to take care of the hungry people?

"How many loaves do you have?" Jesus asked.

How much is in the cupboard? What do you have to use? When the widow of the prophet came and cried out to Elisha because she owed money and the creditor was coming to take her sons as slaves, he asked her, "What do you have in your house?" (2 Kings 4:2). God does not want our children as slaves to inadequacy and lack.

The new move of God will begin with what we have in our house. The Bread of Heaven that they have will be broken and distributed to the dead and dying Church, restoring her to glory. That which they have will be multiplied.

"Seven," they replied.

Again, seven is that number of perfection. Whatever you have will be perfectly sufficient when it is mixed with faith in the Word of God. It is time to reach into the realm of the miraculous to supply whatever need is there. There is no lack in God, for He will supply all of our needs according to His riches in Glory.

He told the crowd to sit down on the ground.

You have to sit down and buckle your seat belt when God takes over. They obediently sat and waited upon the hand of God to provide their needs.

When He had taken the seven loaves and given thanks, He broke them and gave them to His disciples to set before the people, and they did so.

He took what they had, and gave thanks to the Father. Jesus did not see lack; He saw dinner. What they had was perfectly sufficient for the need.

What we have is perfectly sufficient for our needs, when we thank the Father and mix it with faith. God has said He would supply ALL of our needs. He gave the bread to the disciples to distribute. Now, they could have said, "No way! This cannot feed so many, it's impossible!" But they were obedient and passed the plate. When we are obedient, God will meet our needs and fill the baskets with plenty.

They had a few small fish as well; He gave thanks for them also and told the disciples to distribute them.

The fish represent the believers. They were small, but they will meet the need.

We need Jesus, the Bread of Heaven and the Meat of the Word, to eat and be satisfied. With the Word in us, we will be equipped to handle every need of the Church. The power of the miraculous will break through every barrier and supply every need.

We need financial supply to free men and resources for the Kingdom fight. There are many ministries that have dreams, but do not have the money. It is time to learn to reach into the supernatural realm and bring back whatever it is that we lack.

The people ate and were satisfied.

How many satisfied Christians have you met lately? They are fussing and complaining and criticizing. Many have serious problems their pastors are not able to help with. There is a frustration on every level when the baby Christians or demon filled parishioners suction every drop of energy from the pastors and leaders. We need an overcoming power in our lives to break every bond and set the captive free. The people of the Last Days Church will eat and be satisfied. There will be power to break every bond. Those who have been wounded and healed will turn to assist others, and the battle will be won.

Afterward the disciples picked up seven basketfuls of broken pieces that were left over.

Christ not only provided dinner, He provided leftovers. As I was writing about this miracle last Friday, I made a pot of homemade chicken noodle soup. This is a favorite of ours, and I make it

41

frequently. Knowing there was just my husband Gene and me, I planned on making just a small pan for dinner and freeze a bowl full.

As I finished it in the afternoon, I could not believe my eyes as it multiplied. The soup should have filled half of my soup pot, but it grew to within an inch of the top. I chuckled at God's miraculous illustration of His multiplication technique. We had two meals of that soup, and I froze two bowls full instead of one. I especially noticed there was more chicken in it than usual!

When Jesus was done, there were seven baskets of leftovers. Again, that's the number of perfection. God's not only planning to meet our needs; He is going to do it in a big way! There will be miraculous provision in every area. Our God is a God of more than enough.

Straining at the Oars

Jesus walks on the water in Matthew 14:22-33.

Immediately Jesus made His disciples get into the boat and go on ahead of Him to the other side, while He dismissed the crowd.

Jesus commanded His disciples to get into the boat, the Church. When we are saved, we are the

Church. It is not a building; it is Him in us. Jesus stays and dismisses the crowd. Those who came and were fed and healed, but did not acknowledge His Lordship, are dismissed, and the Master physically leaves for the next 2,000 years of Church dispensation.

After He had dismissed them, He went up on a mountainside by Himself to pray.

Jesus will dismiss those who are not truly His disciples. The curious, the uncommitted, those who do not give up themselves and take up their cross. The new move of God that is going to begin will separate those who are true followers from those that do not have a relationship with Him. Jesus has left for the heights of Heaven to commune with His heavenly Father. He has not forgotten His disciples or the people; He is interceding with the Father for them.

When evening came, He was there alone, but the boat was already a considerable distance from land, buffeted by wind the waves because the wind was against it.

The day of this dispensation is ending and the boat of the Church is still in the middle of the lake.

Jesus is alone on the land, but He is coming back again to finish the job.

The Church has been straining. They are making no progress because the wind is blowing them backwards no matter how hard they row. The waters are rough and they are weary. It has been a long difficult night and even though they are attempting to do what Jesus told them to, they are getting nowhere fast.

During the fourth watch of the night Jesus, went out to them walking on the lake.

The fourth watch of the night is actually the morning watch. The Jewish watch was divided into 4 segments of 3 hours each called the even, midnight, the cock crowing and the morning. The disciples have worked and struggled all night, for Jesus saw them from the mountain in the first watch, evening. Three watches are past, and it is into the fourth that Jesus comes. He surprises them, walking on the water. He has commanded us to watch and wait for Him, but it seems He never comes the way we expect Him to!

When the disciples saw Him walking on the lake, they were terrified. "It's a ghost," they said and cried out in fear.

Again, they do not recognize their Master. The mighty Jesus who is Ruler of all nature is not the Jesus they know. He was about to pass them by (Mark 6:48), as He has passed by so many churches today. He has left those who do not recognize the Miracle Worker; He has passed them by. The Church thought the miracles were dead; they have mistaken the Lord of Glory for a ghost. Many will cry out and be terrified because of the mighty wonders of God they will see. The ghost is going to come to life for this Church, and those who want the old dead ways are going to be blown away.

But Jesus immediately said to them: "Take courage! It is I. Don't be afraid."

Jesus is making Himself known to us again. It is time for renewal and restoration of all the Church has lost. It will take courage for the Church to admit she has been wrong, and to change. It will be necessary to eliminate fear, and to go forth with power as this new move of God hits.

"Lord, if it's You," Peter replied, "tell me to come to You on the water."

When we have the guts to say, "If it's you, Lord, tell me to come to You on the water," like Peter did, the miracles will begin. We must recognize that we have the same Jesus that Peter did! He wants us to leave the safety of the boat, and go into the highways and byways with His miracle message. We are supposed to be doing what He did, and more.

"Come," He said.

Every time I read this line, tears fill my eyes. The word from the Lord is "Come." Get up; come to Me all you that are weary and heavy-laden and I will give you rest. Come to My table and eat of Me. My yoke is easy and my burden is light. Come and walk on the water with Me. There will be great joy rising up in the Body as we Come and take possession of His promises.

Then Peter got down out of the boat, walked on the water, and came toward Jesus. But when he saw the wind he was afraid and beginning to sink, cried out, "Lord, save me."

If we learn to eliminate fear – fear of man, fear of the Devil, fear of our inadequacies – we will truly walk on the water with Him. Peter started out great, as did the Church in Acts. For a while the Church was flowing in the miraculous, and began to take over the world. But then, they became afraid. As long as we walk in fear we will sink, and the only thing that can save from fear is Jesus.

Immediately Jesus reached out His hand and caught him. "You of little faith, why did you doubt."

Little faith people will never build His kingdom. As soon as doubt and fear creep in, we are lost. We must step out in the belief that Jesus is the same yesterday, today and forever. As soon as Peter cried out, Jesus reached out His hand and rescued him. It is time the Church cried out with a loud voice for the Master to rescue us from all doubt and fear. Let us get a vision and a passionate desire for the miracles God has prepared for us.

And when they climbed into the boat the wind died down. Then those who were in the boat worshipped Him, saying, "Truly you are the Son of God."

They now recognize Jesus as the miracle worker, the Son of God. When the Last Days Church opens her eyes and sees who Jesus really is, the world will change in an instant. The disciples then worshipped Him, and that is the key to victory. The Church must recognize her Lord and worship Him.

When they had crossed over, they landed at Gennesaret.

They had crossed over with Jesus, and they landed at Gennesaret, which means "garden of riches." The riches and goodness of God are ours when we reach out in faith and take them. There are those in the Body of Christ that are beginning to take those steps of faith into the garden, and when the miracles begin, multitudes will come in with them.

And when the men of that place recognized Jesus, they sent word to all the surrounding country.

The word that the miracle working Jesus is back in business will spread like wildfire among the hurting, wounded, afflicted people who need Him. All of the world can hear in a matter of hours when anything newsworthy happens. When men recognize Him again, the power will flow to the Nations.

People brought all their sick to Him and begged Him to let the sick just touch the edge of His cloak, and ALL who touched Him were healed.

When at a healing crusade or service, there is nothing sadder than those who somehow cannot get quite close enough to touch Him, and leave in their pain. The Church in the Last Days will have services that are so on fire that ALL who come will be healed. Can you imagine the joy and shouting in a service like that? Get ready, it's on the way!

Chapter Three

• The Message in the Miracles of Christ •

Nothing but Leaves

When the fruit of the Spirit ripens in you there will be hungry people flocking to your tree to eat, and they will be filled with the same attributes of the Spirit that are displayed in you.

The miracle of the cursed fig tree (Mark 11:12-25) took place the day after the triumphal entry into Jerusalem. Bethany was the home of Mary, Martha and Lazarus, and Jesus had spent the night there with His disciples, probably at their home.

The next day as they were leaving Bethany, Jesus was hungry.

The Scripture tells us in John 4:34, *"My food,"* *said Jesus, "is to do the will of Him who sent Me* *and to finish His work."* Jesus is hungry because His Father's work is not finished. God started His work in the Garden of Eden, and Jesus came to enable God to finish that work: to destroy the works of satan and restore men to the place for which they were created. He sent Jesus to restore all things. This was no wimpy mission to allow us to warm a pew in a church service on Sunday, and then continue in sin. This was to change us into the image of Christ and to make Earth as Heaven.

Seeing in the distance a fig tree in leaf, He *went to find out if it had any fruit.*

The tree He sees in the distance is the End-Time Church. A fig tree normally has fruit when its leaves are out, so Jesus walks over to pick some.

When He reached it, He found nothing but *leaves, because it was not the season for* *figs.*

54

The tree looks good from a distance, but when Jesus reaches it He finds only leaves, no fruit. Adam and Eve covered their nakedness in the Garden of Eden with fig leaves. They sewed the leaves into clothing by the works of their hands, to cover their unrighteousness. God came and then covered them with the skins of animals, showing that sin can only be covered by the shedding of blood.

The Church has attempted to cover her sin and fruitlessness with leaves, the works of her hands. These have the appearance of godliness, but the fruit of the Spirit is not there. The Spirit leaves that unfruitful place, and goes to the place where He can produce His fruit.

The past 1,800 years have not been the season for figs, because the power of the Spirit has been left out of Church doctrines. The pageants of the Church display the characteristics of the Gospel, but are a stage play. They are missing a personal, vital relationship with God.

Then He said to the tree, "May no one ever eat fruit from you again."

No one can obtain fruit from a dead tree. The fruit of the Spirit is love, joy, peace, patience, kindness, goodness, faithfulness, gentleness and self-control (Gal 5:22-23). Unless you display these attributes in your life, you are not bearing the fruit of the Spirit.

Many times, you hear the teaching that the fruit of your life are those you bring in and "get saved." How many baby Christians have been brought into the Church and then hurt by carnal Christians? If the Spirit of love does not reside in the Church, people come and are wounded. They are eating unripe fruit.

As children, my sister Carine and a friend spent the day sitting in an apple tree eating green fruit. That night I was so grateful I did not play with them, for they were fed some awful pink goop and cried all night with a stomachache. Green fruit hurts, it does not nourish.

When the fruit of the Spirit ripens in you there will be hungry people flocking to your tree to eat, and they will be filled with the same attributes of the Spirit that are displayed in you.

You only get seeds from mature fruit. When your life displays the true fruit, then you will have seeds to sow. Those seeds will prosper and grow under the nourishment of the giver of life.

It says in Matthew 12:33 "Make a tree good and its fruit will be good, or make a tree bad and its fruit will be bad, for a tree is recognized by its fruit." The tree with no fruit is a sad tree indeed. It is worthless, good for nothing except to be burned in the fire.

And His disciples heard Him say it.

Those who have the Word of God and have read it have no excuses. They have the truth straight from the mouth of the Lord, yet they often do not believe. They take their scissors and cut the words out of the Bible that do not follow their philosophies and doctrines. A tree that does not bear the fruit of the Spirit, but simply uses its leaves to cover its nakedness, is cursed, and no fruit will ever be found on it again.

On reaching Jerusalem, Jesus entered the temple area and began driving out those who were buying and selling there. He overturned the tables of the money changers and the benches of those selling doves, and would not allow anyone to carry merchandise through the temple courts. And as He taught them, He said, "Is it not written: 'My house will be called a

57

*house of prayer for all nations?' But you
have made it 'a den of robbers.'"*

The Jewish hierarchy that ran the temple
cheated those that brought the sacrifices to worship
the Lord. They would declare the animal brought
for sacrifice to have an imaginary defect, seize it,
and force the worshiper to purchase one at an
inflated price from them. They then would turn
around and sell the animal that was seized to the
next person. They also required all money to be
converted into temple currency, and cheated the
people in the exchange rates. In reality, the leaders
were keeping the faithful from worship by making it
prohibitively expensive. This was hardest on those
that were poor, and the Lord has continually
commanded us to care for the poor.

Jesus is coming in power and might to clean out
His temple. Our bodies are the temples of the Holy
Spirit, and our leaders have cheated the people out
of their rightful inheritance in Him by teaching false
doctrines. Whenever pieces of the truth are
excluded, the Word is not being taught. The whole
truth of the Gospel must be preached, or the people
are being cheated.

The most severe words from Jesus were to the
religious leaders. And this instance of His anger at

those leaders was because they were interfering with the relationship of the faithful followers, and God must give us pause. Those leaders, who are standing in the way of the message of God through His Word, for whatever reason, are in for a rude awakening when they stand before Almighty God.

The chief priests and the teachers of the law heard this and began looking for a way to kill Him, for they feared Him, because the whole crowd was amazed at His teaching.

At this point, the leaders decided to kill Him, rather than be obedient to God. Throughout history, the leaders of the Church have killed the power of the Gospel by eliminating the miraculous. Their ability to manipulate the worshipers and gain financial prosperity is dependent upon going along with the crowd. They fear the truth of Jesus, because if they get radical, people might leave. If they are preaching an uncomfortable truth to their people, the congregations might kick them out. So they compromise.

Pastors are placed in the Church and ordained by God Almighty, yet we have turned pastoral positions into a popularity contest. A pastor should never be removed because he has offended someone. As a matter of fact, to do their job, they often NEED to offend some people. Jesus was not concerned about hurt feelings when He confronted the religious leaders.

Many parishioners have been blinded by the incomplete Gospel they have been taught. They honestly don't understand the truth or the Living Word. We are coming to a place when the miracles are going to be so obvious, everyone will have to choose sides: tradition and comfort, or truth and risk.

False teaching is no excuse for the followers. With the amount of information available today and ready access to the Word for ourselves, each person is responsible to God for his or her beliefs.

When evening came, they went out of the city.

Evening is here; it is the beginning of the third day. Jesus and his followers leave the city of doubt and disobedience. That city was the abode of those with a form of godliness, but no power. Jesus goes back to the home of the faithful.

In the morning, as they went along, they saw the fig tree withered from the roots.

All of the churches that deny the power of God in these last days will die. They will wither from the roots of their doubt and fear. The faithful that are in them will leave to go to a place where the Living Word is being taught. The Church without the power is over. Its day is done and no one will ever eat fruit of it again.

Peter remembered, and said to Jesus, "Rabbi, look! The fig tree you cursed has withered!"

The leaders will look at the words of Jesus and remember what they meant. They will watch with awe as the Spirit of God moves through and empties the tombs of the dead churches into a vibrant resurrected body of a warrior. The tree that is cursed is withered, but the tree of life has blossomed and is maturing into the final harvest of the End-Times.

It will take more than leaves to make anyone acceptable to the Lord; it will take the fruit of the Spirit.

"Have faith in God," Jesus answered.

The key to all miracles is faith in God. It is the answer to all of our inadequacies and problems. With faith we can truly do all things.

61

Twenty years ago I had two ruptured disks in my lower back. After years of pain and then surgery, I was worse. It was so bad that I had to be hospitalized, and the doctors took another mylegram. The diagnosis was gloomy, and it was too soon for another operation. They sent me home and I laid in bed, with such pain I could only make it to the bathroom and back. My left leg was paralyzed, and I dragged it. There were no reflexes in either foot or in my left leg, and the pain was terrible. With three small children I was desperate, and I prayed for God to heal me. I also prayed that if there was anything standing in the way of my healing, He would reveal it to me.

We went to a Presbyterian Church, but there was a group of Full Gospel people there. One of them called and asked if I would like a book on healing. Of course, I said yes. So, that Sunday, she sent home with my husband Gene the book *New Thresholds of Faith* by Kenneth Hagin.

I read that book all afternoon, and decided if faith is what it took, I was going to find it! I highlighted every verse on faith in my entire Bible, and read them out loud. I dragged my pain-ridden body out of that bed, and got dressed.

I never had anybody pray over me, nor did anyone ever lay hands on me. By faith in the living, breathing Word of God, I was completely healed. It didn't happen in an instant, but that Wednesday night I had improved enough to attend mid-week service. I continued to get better, and at my next doctor's appointment, I had regained my reflexes. He was astonished, for he said that never happens!

I do not limp, nor does my foot drag. I have absolutely no pain, praise God! God is a mighty God, and He finishes what He starts. Faith is the key to activate the power, and astounding miracles will happen when we use faith.

Of course, mighty miracles happen instantly when someone with the anointing lays hands on the sick. The Holy Spirit is working in great power in these last days, and the signs and wonders are just beginning. You can get healed using the faith of the person laying hands upon you, even if you lack it yourself! Whichever way it happens, it still takes faith to activate the miracle.

I tell you the truth, if anyone says to this mountain, "Go, throw yourself into the sea," and does not doubt in his heart but believes that what he says will happen, it will be done for him.

Jesus tells us the truth. The truth is not relative, no matter what your teachers taught you. It is the same yesterday, today and forever. It will stand when all else fails. Anyone who understands the meaning of this verse will have the key to the kingdom. If *anyone* (that means you) *says* (that means to use your mouth and your vocal cords) *to this mountain,* (whatever the mountains are in your life; sickness, debt, poverty, etc.), "*Go, throw yourself into the sea*" (get away from me and disappear underneath the waves of God's love), *and does not doubt in his heart* (do not question God's Word that is placed in your heart) *but believes that what he SAYS will happen* (make sure you understand "you get what you say" so only confess what you want), *it will be done for him* (He does not tell you to get a shovel and move the mountain, it will be done for you!).

Therefore I tell you, whatever you ask for in prayer, believe that you have received it, and it shall be yours.

I have actually heard Christians say, "I don't believe in that faith message." Well, I want to tell them, this is JESUS talking! If you don't believe in what Jesus says, you might as well stay home, watch a game on TV and have another beer, because if you think you're serving God, you are seriously deluded.

Jesus says, *Whatever* (no limitations, no spiritualization, **whatever you want**) *you ask for in prayer* (you need to use your mouth and ask God for whatever...), *believe* (that's "be" and "live" put together) *that you have received it* (it is yours, you have already received it) *and it shall be yours.* Jesus does not hedge or qualify this radical statement. This is God talking here. Whatever you want, ask, believe and receive.

And when you stand praying, if you hold anything against anyone, forgive him, that your Father in heaven may forgive your sins.

Unforgiveness is the greatest burden you can carry and will block everything from the Father's hand. If you are holding unforgiveness in your heart against anyone, forgive them right now. Do not go one more moment walking out of the will of God for you. I don't care what they did, nor do I care what a rotten person they are. That is none of your business. You are to forgive them so God can forgive you.

God never tells us to do something we are unable to do. Forgiveness is not some sweet little warm feeling you get; it is a choice. When you choose to forgive, you activate God's healing power in your life. Simply say, "I forgive you, and I bless you in Jesus name." Every time you think of that person or what they did, say it again. I don't care if it is 100 times an hour, say it again. Eventually you will learn to mean it and you will be cleansed of the memory of it.

There is only one person in the Universe for whom you are responsible, and that is yourself. God may instruct you to witness to someone else, and demand that you obey, but that person is responsible for receiving or denying the Word you give them. Leave the others in God's hand, and keep your temple clean.

There is also a corporate sin that we have committed against the body of Christ. We need to ask forgiveness for the lack of love and acceptance toward those of other denominations who are interpreting Scriptures differently than we are. I am not saying we should compromise the integrity of the Scriptures. I am saying some of the issues that divide the Body are ridiculous. Go back to the Bible and do what it says. I am much more concerned about love for His Body, than I am about doctrinal issues. Let's find what we agree on, and go from there. Much of the rest is unimportant and has been used by the enemy to divide and conquer.

We had a close friend, "Six-Toed" Bill Greenman, who mowed his foot along with his lawn one day. He can tell you first hand of the great pain you cause when you remove one or more of your members – in this case four toes. Think of the pain we cause Jesus when we cut off parts of His Body.

The head controls the body. My knee does not tell my hand what to do. My head tells them both what to do. Ask Jesus to control you, and you will not be concerned what others believe, you will be busy obeying your Head, Jesus.

This ends the power miracles; the next section will be the healing miracles. When we learn to walk in the miraculous, nothing will be impossible for us!

Be Clean

The miracle of healing the man with leprosy is found in Matthew 8:1-4. These miracles need to be taken literally, in that God still is in the healing business, and prophetically, that there is a message in them for the Last Days Church.

When He came down from the mountainside, large crowds followed Him.

Jesus is coming back down the mountain. The Last Days Church is preparing for His return. Large crowds will follow the Jesus that will manifest through this power Church.

A man with leprosy came and knelt before Him,

The Church as it stands is an unclean vessel. It is filled with disease and has been eaten away by sin. As this Church kneels before the Lord and confesses its condition, the miracles will start to happen. It will take recognition of the shape it is in before Christ can manifest in power again. Repentance was John the Baptist's message to prepare the way for the Lord, and that is the message the Church needs today – repentance of pride, self-righteousness, self-seeking, unbelief, doubt of His Word, disobedience to His call – in fact, all sin.

And said, "Lord, if you are willing, you can make me clean.

The Church has cherished her unbelief and doubt, and blamed God for the lack of power in her midst. How many times have you heard, "Well, it must not be God's will..."? This leper says, "IF you are willing, you can." The Church usually believes God has the ability, but does not believe He is willing give her what she needs.

Jesus reached out His hand and touched the man.

Jesus does not hesitate reach out to touch the untouchable, this man who had not been touched in a long time. Lepers were forced to be separated from society and had to cry unclean to prevent anyone else from contracting the disease. How he must have longed for the warmth of the touch of another human. How the Church longs for a touch from Jesus. It is time we were no longer forced to cry "Unclean!" but we realized God has given us the power to be holy and cleansed through the blood of Jesus. We need to bow before him and confess our sins, and yield to His touch.

"I am willing," He said, "Be clean."

Directly from the mouth of God, He sets us straight. He is willing! He is willing to heal us! He is willing to save us! He is willing to sanctify us! He is willing to meet our financial needs! His Word makes it abundantly clear, He is willing!

If there is some need in your life that has not been met, rest assured it is not because there is something wrong with God, or that He is not willing. There is something wrong with your approach. Look at yourself first, and then look at your belief system. What have you been taught? Are you hearing the Word as He wrote it, or is its power being explained away?

Jesus is coming back for a Church that is clean and whole and He has provided the way for that to happen.

Immediately he was cured of his leprosy.

There will be no time wasted as God prepares the Church for the coming of Jesus. After she kneels before Him in true heart repentance and removes the sin from her midst, she will immediately be cleansed of all unrighteousness. Then she will be adorned as a Bride, without spot or wrinkle.

Then Jesus said to him, "See that you don't tell anyone, but go to the priest and offer the gift Moses commanded, as a testimony to them."

Jesus gives us His Word, "Don't tell anyone." I never understood His command to this man, for we need to give thanks and praise to God for what He has done, and be witnesses to man. Then, I realized the gift to be offered is a sacrifice. Jesus is telling this man he has been cleansed and is whole, now give himself back to God as a living sacrifice, and be obedient.

After we are cleansed, we must fulfill the Scriptures and witness unto the unbelieving leaders of the Church. As more and more of the Christians have repented and been filled with the Spirit, they will go to the Church leaders and give their testimony of what God has done. They will show the healings: limbs replaced, cancers gone, heart disease healed, until everyone must make a choice to follow Christ or continue in their religious observations.

Authority

The healing of the Centurion's servant is recorded in Matthew 8:5-13.

When Jesus had entered Capernaum, a centurion came to Him, asking for help.

The word "Centurion" means he was captain over 100 soldiers, and it comes from the same root word as century. The centurion is a Gentile, and centuries later, the Gentile Church needs help desperately, and must come to Jesus and ask.

"Lord," he said, "my servant lies at home paralyzed and in terrible suffering."

The current Gentile Church is paralyzed because of inadequate teaching, which has led to unbelief in the true power of God. There is suffering within the Body of Christ that should not be. Jesus wants to raise up the Church and eliminate her pain.

Jesus said to him, "I will go and heal him."

With compassion, Jesus immediately offers to go and heal this servant. The servant was a Gentile, and Jesus was sent to the Jews, but He is ready to heal those who come to Him.

The Centurion replied, "I do not deserve to have You come under my roof."

This man was a leader of the Roman army, and socially far above Jesus in the culture of that day. He had soldiers and servants under his command, and was feared by the people, but spiritually he recognized his subordinate position. He did not deserve to have the Lord come under his roof. He knew who he was and who Jesus was. Do we?

"But just say the word, and my servant will be healed."

The Church needs to say the Word, and she will be healed. When we learn the power in the Word, then Jesus will come under our roof, and all of our problems will disappear.

"For I myself am a man under authority, with soldiers under me. I tell this one, 'Go,' and he goes, and that one, 'Come,' and he comes. I say to my servant, 'Do this,' and he does it."

This Roman soldier had a perfect grasp of the authority of Christ. He knew perfect obedience to his superior officers, and in turn received perfect obedience from his soldiers. When using the name of Jesus Christ, we have authority to cast out demons, heal the sick, raise the dead and command nature to obey. The very structure of the universe will bow to the Name of Jesus, for He created all things. God has given us the authority to regain the dominion that Adam lost in the Garden of Eden. YOU have the authority of God Almighty backing your every command in His Name.

When Jesus heard this He was astonished, and said to those following Him,

Here is a man who is a Gentile, and is spiritually ahead of all the Jewish followers of Jesus. How I would love to be able to astonish the Lord with my faith! Truthfully though, I'm usually sinking in the water with Peter. Jesus then gives a message to those who follow Him.

"I tell you the truth, I have not found anyone in Israel with such great faith! I say to you, many shall come from the east and the west, and will take their places at the feast with Abraham, Isaac and Jacob in the kingdom of heaven."

It will be those who learn to use the authority of the Name of Jesus and step out in faith doing His works who will take their places at the wedding. It will be a faith crowd who has had dominion restored to them and who reign with Him. They are the rulers over the enemy.

"But the subjects of the kingdom will be thrown outside into the darkness, where there will be weeping and gnashing of teeth."

Those who are the "subjects" rather than "rulers" will be thrown outside. Jesus came to restore the dominion that was lost in the garden. We are not supposed to be "subject" to bondages from which He set us free when He died on the cross. He defeated satan, and when He did, He defeated sickness, poverty and sin.

In the book *The Final Quest,* Rick Joyner sees a vision of the White Throne judgment and is taken to heaven. It is revealed to him in this vision that outer darkness is reserved for those who believed for salvation, but did not follow the highest in Christ. They are the ones who get saved and with a sigh of relief feel that's all there is to it. It is not Hell, and those that were there were happy to have made it to that place, but they are denied the rewards due to those who went on to greater heights.

I do not know the accuracy of Joyner's vision, but the Scriptures clearly teach that there are different levels of rewards in Heaven.

Then Jesus said to the centurion, "Go! It will be done just as you believed it would." And the servant was healed that very hour.

God is always ready and waiting for our faith to kick in. It is done in our lives just as we believe. The Church will be healed the very hour we believe what He told us – no fudging, no excuses – just taking Jesus at His Word. We need to "go" and complete the mission He gave us in Mark 16:15-18:

"Go into all the world and preach the good news to all creation. Whoever believes and is baptized will be saved, but whoever does not believe will be condemned. And these signs will accompany those who believe: In My name they will speak in new tongues; they will pick up snakes with their hands; and when they drink deadly poison, it will not hurt them at all; they will place their hands on sick people and they will get well."

If you say you are a believer, but you are not displaying the signs Jesus gives here, you'd better beware. JESUS said that these signs would accompany believers. In His Name, they will do these things! Every believer is capable of miracles in the Name of Jesus. You need to open yourself up to the highest that God has for you. Praise Him! Love Him! Worship Him! Then get busy and fight for Him.

Your eternal destination is too important to leave to chance. Make sure you look at what the Word says, as opposed to what your doctrine says. Let me tell you, we can't all be right. The only one that is 100% right is Jesus. He is the truth, look to Him for your answers. When we stand before God's throne He is not going to care what your church manual or doctrine says, He is going to ask you why you didn't believe and obey what HE said!

Chapter Four

• The Message in the Miracles of Christ •

A Servant's Heart

There is no greater witness to God's presence in the world than healing.

The Scripture for the miracle of Peter's Mother-in-law is found in Matthew 8:14-17.

When Jesus came into Peter's house, He saw Peter's Mother-in-law in lying in bed with a fever.

Jesus is coming to the leaders, represented here by Peter. A member of Peter's family is sick. The Body of Christ is full of diseases. I don't know of any churches that do not have some sick people in them. I was in the denominational churches when I was filled with the Holy Spirit while reading Benny Hinn's book *Good Morning, Holy Spirit.* I thought when we started going to a Spirit-filled church, there would be no sick members there! Sadly, I was mistaken.

He touched her hand and the fever left her,

Jesus touches her hand. The hand of the Church is the means by which God serves humanity. As soon as Jesus touches her, the fever leaves. Sickness cannot exist in the presence of the Lord, unless we allow it. It says in II Peter 2:24 "By His stripes you were healed." If we are healed, we don't belong in bed with a fever!

And she got up and began to wait on Him.

As soon as Jesus touches us with the reality of His provision for us, we will get up. God has saved us and set us free to serve. We can't serve God lying in a sick bed, we must get up. The Church has allowed satan to blind us to our privileges in Christ to keep us from serving Him and building His kingdom.

When evening came, many who were demon possessed were brought to Him, and He drove out the spirits with a word and healed all the sick

He drove out the spirits with a word. The Scriptures clearly teach that disease is caused by spirits, as well as that it is possible for the human body to be possessed by demon spirits. He healed all the sick, not just a chosen few, not even just those who had enough faith. God loves every human being on the planet. We are His creation and Jesus came to set us free. And Jesus did it with a word.

It says in Genesis 3:14, "So the Lord God said to the serpent, 'Because you have done this, cursed are you above all the livestock and all the wild animals! You will crawl on your belly and you will eat dust all the days of your life.'" This was part of the curse of the fall of man. The serpent was to eat dust, and man is made of the dust of the ground. In this curse, God declared that satan would "eat" man, or cause him to be sick. Microscopic worms and parasites cause most diseases, and worms are tiny snakes, so even in the natural, satan is eating man.

When we go fishing, we use worms for bait. It's time we became proficient at flowing in God's power to heal, and catch some fish on our lines! The Last Days Church will use the diseases, which satan has used to bind people, to bring them in to the kingdom. There is no greater witness to God's presence in the world than healing.

This was to fulfill what was spoken through the prophet Isaiah, "He took up our infirmities and carried our diseases."

Jesus came to defeat the works of the devil. The work that God did through Jesus was complete. Every disease known to man that was eliminated by those stripes. The Word of God is fulfilled in the believer by what that believer speaks.

Wash Those Pigs!

This miracle deliverance of the man from the Gerasenes is recorded in Mark 5:1-20.

They went across the lake to the regions of the Gerasenes. When Jesus got out of the boat, a man with an evil spirit came from the tombs to meet Him.

Jesus is returning to His Church. Whom does He meet, but a man filled with demons. This man comes from the tombs, which is where dead people reside. If you are not a Christian, you are spiritually dead, and possibly demon possessed.

There has never been a time as now that satanism has reared it's ugly head right in the face of the Church in America. Cults, witches, drug usage and open demon worship are prevalent in our society. The secular rock music that pours into our consciousness from every direction screams satan's message. You can't even go shopping without being subjected to loud raunchy lyrics. Drug abuse is rampant.

The thread connecting the violent attacks at our schools by students with guns is satan worship. Each one of the kids that has been involved in the shootings was somehow involved in the occult. The media has chosen to ignore this link, just as society is failing to see what is happening to our young people.

This man lived in the tomb and no one could bind him any more, not even with a chain. For he had often been chained hand and foot, but he tore the chains apart and broke the irons on his feet.

85

The Bible gives us the power to bind demons, but the Church has failed to use it. It says in Matthew 16:19, "Whatever you bind on earth will be bound in heaven, and whatever you loose on earth will be loosed in heaven." We are supposed to be binding satan and his demons. Instead of taking authority over them, the Church has cowered in fear, or denied the existence of such beings.

Today this man would be locked in an insane asylum, probably sedated into incoherence. Locked away, forgotten, these poor souls have no one to break the hold of the enemy on them.

The demonic man in Mark could not be bound, and he represents the failure of the Church to bind demons. Jesus took the keys of authority back from satan, and then gave them to His Body, the Church. The Church is not a cute building with a steeple, it is the people of God. We are to be using the authority Christ gave us to take satan out.

No one was strong enough to subdue him.

The Church has not been strong enough to subdue the enemy. It says in Genesis 1:28, "God blessed them and said to them, 'Be fruitful and increase in number; fill the earth and subdue it.'" Adam failed to obey that command, and as a result satan gained dominion. The Church has had a second chance because of Jesus' victory, and she has failed also. Isn't it time we took God at His word and obeyed Him? We are to be taking dominion of the Earth.

Night and day among the tombs and in the hills he would cry out and cut himself with stones.

Demon possession is a terrible thing. Possession or oppression by demons causes many of the problems we see in people. They get no peace; there is no place of refuge for them. They are the unreasonable ones, those that choose destructive behavior in the face of common sense. It says in the Word, "For our struggle is not against flesh and blood, but against the rulers, against the authorities, against the powers of this dark world, and against the spiritual forces of evil in the heavenly realm" (Eph 6:24).

We are to be the rulers. Jesus defeated satan and took back the keys of authority that satan had stolen from Adam. There is no authority over us but Jesus Christ. There is no power that He did not conquer. It says in Colossians 2:15, "And having disarmed the powers and authorities, he made a public spectacle of them, triumphing over them by the cross." In Jesus we have authority over all other powers. They are defeated, done for, stripped of power, and in submission to us. But we must know that and use it.

Blood line alone does not make a king, he also must have a place for dominion. There are many royal families who were dethroned during World War II, that still are without a country. They have no place to rule, for their kingdom was taken from them. It's about time the Church took the authority Christ gave her, and kicked satan out of our kingdom. He is ruling illegally, and we have the power in Christ to oust him completely.

Let us hear the cry of the possessed and set him free. He cuts himself, hurts himself, because of the demons within him. Jesus came to set the captives free. We must bind the demons to accomplish that.

When he saw Jesus from a distance, he ran and fell on his knees in front of him.

The demons know who Jesus is. This guy sees Him at a distance and recognizes Him immediately. He doesn't walk, he runs to Him.

The people want to be free, and they must fall on their knees before the One who has the power to accomplish that freedom in their lives.

He shouted at the top of his voice, "What do You want with me, Jesus, Son of the Most High God? Swear to God that You won't torture me!"

The name of Jesus puts terror in the heart of demons, and they panic at the mention of the blood! We have power through Jesus Christ to cast them out and send them to the dry places if we choose. The King James Version says, "What have we to do with Thee, Jesus, Thou Son of God? Art Thou come hither to torment us before the time?" The demons know their time here is limited, and with the imminent return of Christ, I believe their time is up.

For Jesus had said to him, "Come out of this man, you evil spirit!"

Jesus immediately commands the demon to come out. He came to set the captives free. The demons start trying to bargain with Jesus to determine their destination. There is no doubt on the part of the demons that they must leave this man; they just are trying to negotiate their next stop.

Then Jesus asked him, "What is your name?" "My name is Legion" he replied, "for we are many."

Knowing the demons name seems to help to cast it out. Take authority over them and command them to leave. In the name of Jesus they must obey you.

And he begged Jesus again and again not to send them out of the area.

The same miracle recorded in Luke 8:31 in the King James Version says, "And they begged Him not to command them to depart into the abyss," which means "perishing, destruction" in the Greek, and the root word of it means Hades. They were begging Jesus not to send them to Hell, for in that dispensation it was not yet time.

A large herd of pigs was feeding on the nearby hillside. The demons begged Jesus, "Send us among the pigs; allow us to go into them."

If you ever wondered how people become possessed with demons, here is your answer. Pigs are unclean animals, and they were feeding on garbage. Pigs do not graze; this was probably the garbage dump for the local area. Pornography, adultery, lies, cheating, wife and child abuse, self-seeking, homosexuality, gossip, demonic video games – the garbage human spirits feed upon is endless.

He gave them permission, and the evil spirits came out and went into the pigs.

Physical garbage dumps attract vermin; spiritual garbage dumps attract demons. You can't play with sin and expect to stay clean. They have permission to enter those who are unclean.

Sexual sins are the worst. Homosexuality is a demon that is attached to a human being during sex with a person who is infected. This is often spread by child abuse, so it is extremely important to keep your kids in a protected environment. Do not let them spend the night with people you do not know well, and never with anyone who is not a Christian. This includes friends from school and birthday parties. Do not allow your children to be alone with family members with whom your spirit does not feel comfortable. It is your job to keep them safe.

The herd, about 2,000 in number, rushed down the steep bank into the lake and were drowned.

For 2,000 years the Church has failed to take a stand against the demons, and believe the Word of

God. Satan is still saying to the Church as he did to Eve, "Did God really say...?" As the Church stands up in this last hour of the last day, and takes authority over the demons, the unclean will rush to the water of the Holy Spirit, die to themselves and be cleansed.

Those tending the pigs ran off and reported this in the town and countryside and the people went out to see what happened.

There are those making a great living off of the pigs. Wherever there is garbage you will also find the rats. Drug lords and movie moguls, TV producers and scandal sheets, Pimps and record producers. The list is endless. They are going to immediately get the people into an uproar about their losses when the restoration hits.

When they came to Jesus, they saw the man who had been possessed by the legion of demons, sitting there, dressed and in his right mind; and they were afraid.

The unclean are not comfortable with the clean. They are looking at this man, now healed, trying to figure out what is going to happen when this thing spreads, and sin no longer makes the cash register ring. When they can't use the possessed for their own pleasures any more. Fear grips the populace as they see God taking over lives that had been given to sin.

Those that had seen it told the people what had happened to the demon-possessed man – and told about the pigs as well.

People started talking. Any time God begins to move, there will be those who come against it. The blessing of setting this man free is entirely lost in the midst of the tale bearing and fear. Satan gets busy when his power is threatened, but there is no reason to be afraid of him. Greater is He that is in us than he that is in the world.

You are teamed with the greater One. When we were kids and choose up sides for a game, we always wanted to be on the side with the winners, the strong, athletic kids. Well, God's side always wins!

Then the people began to plead with Jesus to leave their region.

When revival hits, there will be many that will ask Jesus to go. They won't see their own needs, nor want a God of power to take over their lives. They liked those pigs, and in fact, profited by them. It could even be that they are one!

As Jesus was getting into the boat, the man who had been demon-possessed begged to go with Him. Jesus did not let him, but said, "Go home to your family and tell them how much the Lord has done for you, and how He has had mercy on you."

Jesus wants us to get free, and then free our families. We have to go home and make them understand how much God has done and how merciful He is. The break-up of the family is the greatest tragedy of this century. We are reaping the results in crime, suicide, juvenile delinquency and social ills of every description.

So the man went away and began to tell in the Decapolis how much Jesus had done for him. And all the people were amazed.

There's no testimony quite so effective as a completely changed life. As people are healed and set free, all who know them will be amazed. Multitudes will come to resolve the problems in their lives.

We are His disciples just as much as Peter and John were. When Jesus called them in Matthew 10:1 He "gave them authority to drive out evil spirits and to cure every kind of disease and sickness." As a believer you have that same authority. It is time to learn how to use it.

There is not space here for "how to get rid of demons," but get a good book like *The Bondage Breaker* by Neil Anderson, or *Strongman's His Name...What's His Game?* by Drs. Jerry and Carol Robeson. The most important thing to learn is you are the boss, and the demons MUST obey you.

Get up!

We are taking the miracle of the paralyzed man from the second chapter of Mark, verses 1-12.

A few days later, when Jesus again entered Capernaum, the people heard that He had come home.

Jesus is coming back soon. The miracles always seem to start with His return. He had done many signs and wonders by this time and the word had spread. Suddenly, even His neighbors and friends in Capernaum were crowding in to hear Him. Those who have been familiar with Jesus and thought they knew Him will begin to hear new stories of signs and wonders. They will get hungry for the true Christ of power and begin to crowd in.

So many gathered that there was no room left, not even outside the door, and He preached the word to them.

The people have come around to hear the Word of God. Suddenly, in many churches the true Word is being preached. Jesus is placed back in their midst, and the crowds are beginning to come to listen.

Some men came, bringing to him a paralytic, carried by four of them.

A paralyzed person is not responding to the commands from his brain to his body. He is unable to move when his head tells him to move. That is the state of the Church – they have not listened to the Head, and thus, they have been disconnected from their command center.

This man, carried in by his friends, represents the state of the unresponsive Church. She cannot move and is unable to carry out the mission of the building of the kingdom.

This guy was lucky, though, for he had friends. As the restoration begins, those that are made whole will need to carry in those that are still paralyzed. The entire Body needs to be healed and come into the fullness of God.

Since they could not get him to Jesus because of the crowd, they made an opening in the roof above Jesus and, after digging through it, lowered the mat the paralyzed man was lying on.

The crowds around Jesus were so thick, they couldn't get near. The friends of the paralytic are a perfect example of people who are really hungry for God. There is nothing that is going to stop them. If they couldn't get in one way, they would find another.

The path the Church has taken for the last 2,000 years has not worked too well. We can't get close enough to touch the real Jesus. We know He's there, and we've heard He can heal. It's time to go through the roof – to climb higher and grab a hold of the truths in Scripture that the crowds have not grasped. Let's get that kind of hunger for God that NOTHING will stand in our way!

These friends lower the mat with this immobile man on it, right in Jesus' face.

When Jesus saw their faith, He said to the paralytic, "Son, your sins are forgiven."

They came to Jesus and believed in Him and His message. Jesus recognized this man's real need, which was to have his sins forgiven. When you see Jesus, you see the true needs of your soul. It's like looking into a spiritual mirror, and the reflection reveals the condition of your heart. The need for the Church is to have faith in Jesus to forgive their sins. It is time to fall on her face in repentance.

Now some teachers of the law were sitting there, thinking to themselves, "Why does this fellow talk like that? He's blaspheming! Who can forgive sins but God alone?"

According to the religious leaders, Jesus was way off base. They looked and saw this man who had to be carried around and couldn't move, and Jesus is talking about forgiving sin. They thought they had sin all figured out – and God all figured out. If anyone wanted to come to God, it had to be through them. They believed they were the only ones who knew the law and what God wanted.

Immediately Jesus knew in His spirit that this was what they were thinking in their hearts, and He said to them, "Why are you thinking those things?"

"As a man thinketh in his heart, so is he." What gives some leaders the gall to figure their way is the only way, rather than God's way is the only way? They think they have it all figured out, and yet deny pieces of God's Word. Pride is the greatest barrier to God's presence. The Jewish leaders were a proud people, and the Church today is full of pride. Look at what we have, look at how religious we are, look at how wrong they are, look, look, look.... Why are they thinking those things instead of putting the Word of God to life in themselves?

Which is easier: to say to the paralytic, "Your sins are forgiven," or to say, "Get up, take your mat and walk"? But that you may know that the Son of Man has authority on earth to forgive sins....

The Church needs forgiveness of its sins before it will be healed. Its paralysis is caused by the failure to heed the Word of God and obey what it says. God has called the Church to be holy, set apart for His work in this world. The Church is the hand of God moving on the earth. It must be a clean hand to accomplish the task that has been laid out for this day. Jesus has the authority to forgive our sins, and when we are forgiven....

He said to the paralytic, "I tell you, get up, take up your mat, and go home." He got up, took his mat and walked out in full view of them all.

It is a forgiven, healed Church that Jesus is telling to go home. That Church will get up and walk in full view of the world; strong and filled with life. It will no longer be carried around or lying down on the job, but will finally accomplish God's will here on earth.

This amazed everyone and they praised God, saying, "We have never seen anything like this!"

When Christ rises up in the Church for this last day, everyone will indeed be amazed. They shall see signs and wonders such as have not been seen since Jesus walked the earth. There will be miracles and healing and deliverance. God is about to move on our behalf.

Chapter Five

Let's Press In

Jesus is looking for a personal relationship with each of us.

This miracle is about the woman with the issue of blood. We are taking the Scripture from Mark 5:24-34.

Jesus was at a dinner at Matthew's house when He was interrupted by a desperate father. Every one left the party and went to watch Jesus heal Jairus's little girl. On the way, this second miracle occurs. We will cover the raising of Jarius's daughter from the dead in Chapter 9.

So Jesus went with him. A large crowd followed and pressed around Him.

The living Jesus attracts crowds wherever He goes. These people were pressing in around Him to get closer. When the fire of God lights in your heart and you see the real Jesus, the mighty Son of God who has power to take away your problems, you press in. You get as close as you possibly can.

Jesus is always there and always willing to fill you with power, but you have to push away the things that crowd Him out of your life. Turn off the TV. Stay home from the mall. Give up the petty things that eat at you. Get out of bed early and pray. Take time to worship and pray every day. There is a crowd keeping you from the Master until you decide to make Him the center of your life. Then, it's easy to let loose of all else and press in to touch Him.

And a woman was there who had been subject to bleeding for twelve years.

This woman was "subject" to bleeding. This issue of blood would have prevented her from worshiping at the temple, for she was unclean. This was keeping her from God. She was under satan's dominion, subject to him rather than God.

The people of God are created to rule. We have dominion over satan, and we are ordered to take authority in Jesus' Name. Believing in the Name gives us the ability to eliminate those things in our lives that are keeping us from our Father in Heaven.

She had suffered a great deal under the care of many doctors and spent all she had, yet instead of getting better she grew worse.

The suffering around us is incredible. My father had cancer when I was a child and was ill for 20 years before he died. Because of radiation burns to treat the cancer, he had to have multiple operations including skin grafts, and was in constant pain. All of the family resources went to pay for medical services that made him worse. No one knows better than I that doctors can create other problems more serious than those which they attempt to cure. Many diseases have no known cure. The fourth leading cause of death in the United States is adverse reactions to prescription drugs.

This woman spent herself trying to get well outside of God. She did everything she knew, impoverished herself, and was still sick – still unclean.

When she heard about Jesus, she came up behind Him in the crowd and touched His cloak,

The anointing covers us as a cloak. It is a robe that is very real. Jesus walked in the anointing in a greater measure than anyone since, but He has said we will do what He did. The anointing oil in the Old Testament was poured over the person's head, and it would flow down their body to their feet. Jesus is our Head, and that anointed covering pours down from Him over His Body.

It was this covering of the Holy Spirit into which this woman tapped. Clothing can actually be saturated with the anointing, and then it can be transferred to others like Paul did with his handkerchiefs.

Because she thought, "If I just touch his clothes, I will be healed."

She recognized the healing power in Jesus, and understood that if she could just get close enough to touch Him, she would be healed. The Church is beginning to see the real Jesus again. Thousands of people have been healed. But there are still those who have the message without the power. They see that Jesus sometimes heals, but they don't believe it is for everyone. There are also those that believe the day of miracles is over.

This woman knew in her spirit that this healing was for HER! She pushed and shoved and displayed totally unladylike behavior, not caring who saw her or what they thought. She had her healing in sight, and she was grabbing it.

In Matthew 9:20 (King James Version), it says she "touched the hem of His garment." We see in Isaiah 6:1, "I saw the Lord seated on a throne, high and exalted, and the train of His robe filled the temple." We have more than a touch of the hem of that garment inside of us. We are the temple of the Lord, and His train fills us! There is more than enough in there to heal every disease, cast out every demon, and provide every need for every person on the face of the planet.

Immediately her bleeding stopped and she felt in her body that she was freed from her suffering.

What relief Jesus brings! What a joy to live without pain. She knew that her suffering was over. The Church is beginning to press in. As she does, she will be relieved from her suffering. She will at last be restored to the place that God has set for her. It is time to begin her rule.

At once Jesus realized that power had gone out from Him. He turned around in the crowd and asked, "Who touched My clothes?"

The power is the Holy Spirit that flows from Jesus by orders of the Father. It will flow into all that reach out to be cleansed. You must press in and eliminate everything that would crowd in to distract or burden you.

You see the people crowding against You," His disciples answered, "and yet You can ask, "Who touched Me?" But Jesus kept looking around to see who had done it.

Jesus is looking for a personal relationship with each of us. Even though there are 6 billion souls on this planet, He is interested in each one of us. When we reach out to touch Him He will not fail to notice. He will meet that need the moment we make contact.

Then the woman, knowing what happened to her, came and fell at His feet and, trembling with fear, told Him the whole truth.

When the Church realizes what has happened to her, looks at her condition and touches Jesus, she will be filled with power and healed. Then she shall fall at His feet, trembling with fear in the presence of Jesus the King. At this point she will be able to tell the WHOLE truth, not just the part with which she was comfortable. The Full Gospel will be preached from every yielded pulpit in the land, for God will pour out His truth and nothing shall stand in His way.

He said to her, "Daughter, your faith has healed you, go in peace and be freed from your suffering."

It is faith that presses in until the manifestation of His presence brings healing. When we are healed, we will go in His peace, free from our suffering. The back problems I mentioned earlier have given me a great appreciation of healing and the blessing of a pain free life. Just as He has healed me physically, He has healed me emotionally. He has taken the hurts and poured His great love upon me, until I rest in the peace and joy of His love.

I long for the day the Church will be filled to over-flowing with His peace. No fighting, no hurt feelings, no offended people walking off in a huff. When you live in His love, there is no room for self, and it is only the self that gets offended. If you are walking in hurts, take them to the Master and start forgiving. When you forgive, the healing comes.

Have Mercy on Us, Lord

The miracle of the two blind men is only found in Matthew 9:27-31.

As Jesus went on from there, two blind men followed Him, calling out, "Have mercy on us, Son of David."

The two blind men who are following Jesus represent the two large divisions of His Church, the Catholic church and the Protestant church. Jesus has only one Body, and it is the Church. You can label the parts of your body, and indeed we do, but if you cut your body in half you are going to be dead. Both halves of the Church of Jesus Christ are blind to the truth of one Body. It is through His Body God's work is to be done here on earth, and I never saw anyone with only half a body accomplish anything.

Is it any wonder they are crying for mercy? It is Jesus, Son of the Jewish King David, who leads ery believer under the same banner. The time has

110

come to put away divisive denominational issues and get on with the work of building His kingdom.

The true issue is not what label you place on the part of your body you are using, but to whom you have pledged your allegiance. Is it to Christ, Son of the Living God, or to a tradition or creed?

It is time we, who follow Him, realize how blind we are and call out to Him, that He might have mercy on us.

When He had gone indoors, the blind men came to Him, and He asked them, "Do you believe that I am able to do this?"

Jesus is inside of us, and we must come to Him there. He wants to know if we believe that He is able to heal and restore us. Our biggest problem is that we always think it's the other guy that is blind to the truth.

It is those who are saying they are not blind, who need to look at what Jesus said to the religious Pharisees of His day in Matthew 23. We all have blind spots, especially in the denominational issues. Any doctrine that has Scripture leading to the left when another Scripture tends to lead to the right probably has a correct interpretation down the middle. Don't lean on what you've been taught;

lean on God and His Word. Listen to His voice and you will not fall off the path. Always keep an open mind, centered on the Scriptures.

The Lord told me the Scripture is like a child's building block. One side says "A" while the other side might read "Z." Both are true. We tend to only read the side to which we are exposed, closing our minds to the other side of the truth.

"Yes, Lord," they replied.

I'm sure those words are like music to God's ears. "Yes, Lord. Yes, You are able. Yes, we will obey You. Yes, we will honor You by maintaining a holy life. Yes, we want Your will instead of our own."

We need to understand that God is willing and able to heal us when we come to Him. We attended several denominational churches over the years, because Gene moved a lot with his work. We learned doctrine from one, and then found the doctrine from another would be in direct conflict. We finally decided they were all a little confusing, and just did our best to walk in love and believe the Word.

We said "Yes" to God and forgot about the rest. It really doesn't matter, as long as you have the basics of salvation down correctly, and you faithfully study the Word. There are actually more issues upon which we all agree than those upon which we don't. Let's start saying "yes" to the things where we agree. We believe that He is able to keep His Body in perfect order.

Different parts of the physical body have different functions. Different denominations have different assignments in the building of the Kingdom of God. Some are better soul winners, some are better Bible teachers, some have more anointing, etc. This Last Days Church is going to take every church that is willing to say "yes" to Him and make it a mighty force in the last move of God.

Then He touched their eyes and said; "According to your faith will it be done to you." And their sight was restored.

Jesus will touch the eyes of His Body according to her faith, and at last her sight will be restored. What that Body of believers will see is the might and power of the resurrected King, working through them to finish the Father's will on earth. The things to which we have been blind will be restored to us through faith. Read the book of Acts and catch the vision.

Jesus warned them sternly, "See that no one knows about this.

The problems in the Body are not to be broadcast to the four winds. When we know there is an issue in the lives of some brother or some church, we need to take it to God, not to Primetime Live or even TBN. Let's start building each other up rather than tearing down. Be especially careful once God has opened your eyes, that you do not turn around to accuse others of being blind. Let's love our brothers in Christ. Teach by what you live, not what you say.

But they went out and spread the news about Him all over that region.

Of course, when miracles start happening it is going to be difficult to keep it quiet. The excitement of your revelation is almost contagious. It is important that all of the news of the next move of God is spread in love and not condemnation.

Speak Up

The miracle of this demon possessed man is recorded only once in Matthew 9:32-33. It follows the miracle of the two blind men.

While they were going out, a man who was demon-possessed and could not talk was brought to Jesus.

The disciples were with Jesus and another mute, demon-possessed person is brought to Him. This man represents the Church today that is not speaking for Him. You cannot speak for God when you are filled with the devil's words. Those doctrines filled with doubt and unbelief must go before the Church can stand up and speak again.

There are many that are ministers of the present day churches that do not even confess salvation. It is time to get back to the basics of the teachings of Christ. We need to be absolutely certain that the basic tenants of our faith are founded upon God's complete Word.

And when the demon was driven out, the man who had been mute spoke.

When we are clean and demon-free and filled with the Spirit, we can speak for Him. When the Church is back to where she belongs and has repented of the errors and sin afflicting her, she will stand up and speak for Jesus Christ. The miracles will begin to flow with a mighty anointed power. Every gift of the Spirit will increase and we will see the Church of Acts revived.

The crowd was amazed and said, "Nothing like this has ever been seen in Israel.

The power and glory of the Church in Acts amazed Israel, but most of the Jews still did not follow the Lord. Let us pray for a greater day than they saw. A mightier wind is blowing, a stronger power is coming forth, for God Almighty has declared His Word, and the last day shall exceed the former. We shall go home victorious, without spot or wrinkle, washed in the blood of the lamb.

Jesus is not coming back for a defeated remnant of His people, He is coming back for a glorious Church, worthy to be called His Bride.

Reach Out

The healing of the man with the shriveled hand takes place in Mark 3:1-5.

Another time He went into the synagogue, and a man with a shriveled hand was there.

This miracle happened when Jesus was in the House of God. The man with the shriveled hand represents the work of God through the Church.

The Church is the hand of God in the world. It is shriveled and unable to accomplish the mission God has laid out for it.

Some of them were looking for a reason to accuse Jesus, so they watched Him closely to see if He would heal him on the Sabbath.

It's obvious in the eyes of these religious people that healing is needed here, but they only want it on their terms. They are looking for an excuse to accuse. They are watching to make sure that nothing happens outside of their plans and programs. The have made a law unto themselves, and all must follow their way or not be allowed to touch God.

God does not work through man-made laws and traditions. His power is sacred, and no man can usurp it. The last move of God tends to solidify in the hearts of men and become tradition, and at that point will stand against the next move of God. Man forever looks to attempt to remove God's power unto himself.

Jesus said to the man with the shriveled hand, "Stand up in front of everyone."

Jesus wants the Church to stand up before all, and show her condition. The shriveled hand of tradition is useless. It serves to sever men from God rather than to bring them in. That's why God must continue to move in fresh ways, to break through the leaders who have turned their hearts to stone. They either will fall and break upon the Rock, or the Rock will fall upon them and crush them.

Then Jesus asked them, "Which is lawful on the Sabbath: to do good or to do evil, to save life or to kill?"

The law is death, but the Spirit is life. The Church must choose life so the Spirit can begin to work through Her. It is the job of the Church to bring life to a dying world, healing to a hurting people, prosperity to the poor and hungry, deliverance to the oppressed. This can only be accomplished through the complete work that God has ordained.

But they remained silent.

The Church has been silent while the government allowed millions of infants to die through abortion. She has remained silent while prayer was taken out of our schools. She has remained silent while liberals perverted the media and distorted the news. She has remained silent when sin was found in her midst. She has remained silent to the needs of a dying people around the globe.

When God's Word is standing before the Church, she must not remain silent. She must lift up the standard of perfection God has laid out for His people.

He looked around at them in anger and, deeply distressed at their stubborn hearts, said to the man,

The wrath of God is not something I want to face. Jesus is angry at the stubborn hearts of the people. All of those who fail to follow His directions will be in the path of God's wrath. I don't know how many times I asked my children, "What did I say?" when they were young.

God has given us a directive to love His people, and in fact, to love our enemies. We are to live clean and holy lives. We are supposed to be getting our orders from God Almighty and then doing what He told us to do. If we do not, we are in rebellion.

"Stretch out your hand."

When Moses came to the Red Sea, he cried out to God in prayer. His enemies were close at his heels, and the mountains had hemmed him in on both sides. The only way out was through the water, and he had custody of millions of people. I would have prayed too.

But God was angry with his prayer. God told him to use the rod He had given him, and stretch out his hand. When Moses obeyed, the sea parted. God wants us to use the authority He has given us in the Name of Jesus Christ. That Name is our rod, it is our scepter. When we use it, the sea will part for us.

He stretched it out, and his hand was completely restored.

As the Church stretches out her hand in faith and obedience, she will be completely restored. God is ready to do great and mighty miracles in this last day, for the Church Jesus comes to pick up for the wedding will be perfect.

We need a whole Body to do His work. There is much to be accomplished before the great and mighty day of the Lord. It will take the strength of every believer to do the work. Let us stretch our hand out in faith, to be empowered, and then finish the job He has set out for us to do. It is after all, the least we can do for the One who gave us all.

The Strong Man

The miracle deliverance of the demon-possessed blind and mute man is found in Matthew 12:22-29.

Then they brought Him a demon-possessed man who was blind and mute, and Jesus healed him, so that he could both talk and see.

They bring to Jesus a man who was demon-possessed and could not see or speak. This man represents the Church, which as we have discussed, is both blind and unable to speak. Jesus is about to change all of that. Satan has blinded us to demon activity to prevent us from using the weapons God has placed in our hands to defeat them, and our greatest weapon is speaking His Word.

One thing on which the Church has had limited knowledge is demon possession. During the inquisition there was tremendous persecution on prophets and those who taught the supernatural. Anyone who even discussed these issues was at risk of prison, torture and death. This, of course, prevented any study of the kingdom of darkness, and the existence of demons was placed in the realm of the mythical. Well, Jesus is God, and if he says there are demons, we'd better listen.

121

All the people were astonished, and said,
"Could this be the Son of David?"

As the Church recognizes who Jesus really is, many will be astonished. They know a lot about Jesus, but have not met Him in a personal way.

"The Son of David" speaks of Jesus' kingship; it is as King of Kings and Lord of Lords that He will be known when He comes again. Some have been born again, but do not know the Lord as King. The people must recognize Jesus as their Master and King.

But when the Pharisees heard this, they
said, "It is only by Beelzebub, the prince of
demons, that this fellow drives out demons.

The leaders who trust in tradition and are enjoying their power will not recognize Jesus as Master and King. Every new move of God is attributed to satan. If those leaders said that Jesus was dealing with satan, the leaders today are surely going to say it about us, when we come against the powers of darkness.

Jesus knew their thoughts and said to
them, "Every kingdom divided against itself
will be ruined, and every city or household
divided against itself will not stand.

As long as the Church is divided, she cannot be the force that is needed to defeat satan. She must stand together with all of her members intact to fight the fight that is coming up between the Kingdom of Light and the kingdom of darkness.

As individuals, we must make sure our hearts are centered on the Lord. If you have questions about issues, go to the Word. Be sure you are in a Church Body that is teaching the unadulterated Word of God. If you are divided, you cannot stand up for Christ.

There must also be corporate unity in the Body of Christ. Different denominations have been established, but if they are believers, they are your brothers and sisters. We need to unite on a corporate level to give us the power we need to accomplish God's work.

If satan drives out satan, he is divided against himself. How then can his kingdom stand?

The Lord is telling us what we must do to preserve a spiritual kingdom. It is our responsibility to build and protect the kingdom of God upon the earth.

The Church needs to realize she must be united to stand. Every thing that comes against the Body of Christ to tear and destroy is from satan. We must look at the Word of God for all truth and forget about shooting down our brothers. If we spent one tenth of the energy working on our own relationship with God that we do checking out what others are up to, the kingdom of God would jump ahead a few hundred light years. So many times, we focus on others mistakes to keep everyone from looking at ours or deal with them ourselves. We tend to compare ourselves, saying, "I'm not so bad, look at what so-and-so is doing.

And if I drive out demons by Beelzebub, by whom do your people drive them out? So then, they will be your judges.

Those who are spiritually astute enough to recognize demons and drive them out will be the judges of those who sit in their intellectual seats and sneer at the warriors of God. It doesn't take great learning and a Bible school education to drive out a demon. It takes a belief in the authority of the Name of Jesus and recognition of the power of the blood, which has overcome them.

Book knowledge can serve to separate us from God, as well as bring us closer. The Pharisees were learned men, the most educated of their day, but they were spiritually dead. Jesus chastised them and called them all sorts of names.

A title in front of your name, or a graduate degree from a prestigious theological seminary is no guarantee of a relationship with God Almighty. It may just be an avenue for pride to enter, and the enemy will destroy the ministry God had planned for your life.

But if I drive out demons by the Spirit of God, then the kingdom of God has come upon you.

When we get rid of the demons, the kingdom of God will come upon the Church. It is His Spirit in our mouth that will drive every demon from our door. We will establish His kingdom – His glorious Church without spot or wrinkle.

I was grieving in prayer over some of the people in our church that have been bound by demons and are unwilling to be set free. As I asked the Lord about it He told me that, "The day is coming soon when the demons shall leave instantly, or the people that want to keep them will run from your presence screaming."

Or again, how can anyone enter a strong man's house and carry off his possessions unless he first ties up the strong man? Then he can rob his house.

This Scripture is an example of the blindness in the Body of Christ interpreting God's Word. I had always been taught the strong man was satan. The Lord told me the Christian is the strong man. God would not use the example of a thief to represent His precious children. He also would not build up satan's ego by calling him a strong man. It took me about four times reading this passage before I grasped what the Lord was saying in my Spirit.

Satan ties up the Church by sin, deception and tradition with the multitudes of things that bind men. We allow him to deceive us and blind us to the truth until we are so tied up that satan can come into our house and steal our blessings. Take out that letter "L" and blind becomes bind.

God has given us weapons to bind satan and his demons and prevent him from stealing from us. Unless we open our eyes and speak the Word, we allow him to come in and take what God has provided for us. The blind and mute person in this miracle is a perfect picture of what the Church has allowed satan to do to her.

The other version of this same miracle can be found in Luke 11:21-22:

When a strong man, fully armed, guards his own house, his possessions are safe. But when someone stronger attacks and overpowers him, he takes away the armor in which the man trusted and divides up the spoils.

This obviously identifies the strong man as the Christian. We must guard what God has given us from the enemy. It states we are safe as long as we are fully armed and guarding our house. Satan is not stronger than we are, for greater is He that is in us than he that is in the world.

We sin and play around until things get hot, and then go crying to God to rescue us. In His mercy, He does that, but we have been robbed of the blessings God has planned for us.

Notice it says in this passage that "he takes away the armor in which the man trusted and divides up the spoils." When satan comes in, he attempts to steal the Word that God has placed in our hearts. The spoils are all of the blessings God wants for you. Satan will take your family, your money and possessions, your health and your faith if you let him. He will spoil God's plan for you.

It's back to the garden again with Eve where satan whispered, "Did God really say..." The Word gives us the weapons to fight satan and provides the armor to protect us from his attacks. We must not allow satan to come in and rob us of that Word. Adam was supposed to guard the garden.

God has given us everything we need to fight the enemy in His Word. There are verses we need to memorize and get down into our Spirit so we can fight the enemy when he comes.

It has been a great revelation to me that I am the strong man. What a joy to know that if I live a clean and holy life and keep that armor on, nothing can come against me. I am home to the Greater One!

Chapter Six

The Children's Bread

The Church has taken the living bread of Jesus, and removed all of the power from it, then given it out as a placebo depleted of all nourishment.

Jesus' remark about the children's bread can be found in Matthew 15:21-28.

Leaving that place, Jesus withdrew to the region of Tyre and Sidon.

This region was not even in the country of Israel, but in Phoenicia, which was north of Galilee. It was a country that had been severely criticized by the prophets for its idol worship and heathenism.

The word "withdrew" in the Scripture implies He was taking a rest from the crowds, possibly to have some time to teach His disciples. In Mark 7:24 it is revealed that He was trying to keep His presence there a secret.

He has left the area of His assignment, and is now on Gentile land. The Church is Gentile territory for the most part, although I believe the original plan of God would have been for the Jewish people to take the leadership of the Church to the nations, and rule them under God. The Jews were the seed that would produce God's kingdom on earth. Whenever we fail to take the land you can be certain that satan and his crowd is going to move in.

A Canaanite woman from that vicinity came to Him, crying out, "Lord, Son of David, have mercy on me! My daughter is suffering terribly from demon-possession."

This woman represented the people that the Israelites failed to remove from the land God gave them. They are idol worshipers and a heathen nation, cursed under the law. They represent sin in the camp, and the Church is full of Canaanites. They are suffering from demon-possession, because they have worshiped and partaken of the world system. They have compromised with and served the enemy.

> *Jesus did not answer a word. So His disciples came to Him and urged Him, "Send her away, for she keeps crying out after us."*

Jesus has already given the Church His Word. He is not coming in and changing it to allow us to sin and still live in the Promised Land. When you fail to meet the standards, you move outside of the camp of the redeemed. God will not give a special word for those who have failed to keep His Word, rather, they will be judged by that Word.

The Church is crying for a new word, a word to take care of the problems that are overwhelming them. They want to get rid of the demons, to take satan's hand off of their lives, but they must go back to the Word that God has already provided. The leaders are crying for help in dealing with the increased wickedness of the age and their inability to deal with the hurt and broken people in the congregations.

He answered, "I was sent only to the lost sheep of Israel."

Jesus was focused upon His mission, which was to the house of Israel. To them He was sent and His obedience to God's plan did not allow for deviations. We, as a Body of believers, need to refocus on God's plan for His kingdom on earth. It is to take the land He has given us, and obey the Word He has given us.

Every believer is not a pastor, but every believer has a ministry. We must not allow ourselves to be pulled from the ministry God has given us into another area without His specific direction. If you are in the ministry God has assigned you, the anointing will flow. If you are outside of that ministry, even for another good work, it is of the flesh and you are not under the anointing. Those who do not yet know what their ministry is should be in the ministry of helps, to which we are all assigned.

When we become involved in social programs, no matter how pretty or high sounding they may seem, we are in danger of losing the vision of our true mission. There is a zillion things that can and do to distract us from the true kingdom work. No matter how legitimate a program, if it takes God's time, it is a sin.

The woman came and knelt before Him. "Lord, help me!"

Let's get down on our knees before Him, and spend time in prayer. We need direction for ourselves and corporate prayer for our congregations to know God's plan. We need His help to equip the army of warriors needed for this final hour.

He replied, "It is not right to take the children's bread and toss it to their dogs."

The bread belongs to the children. Jesus is the bread of life, and that life is our right as children of God. He has provided salvation, healing and abundance for us in Jesus. This bread belongs to us, yet we scatter it like swill for the pigs or food for the dogs. The Church has taken the living bread of Jesus, and removed all of the power from it, then given it out as a placebo depleted of all nourishment.

When my children were little, two of them had allergies, so I got them on health food to try to help them. Junk food was eliminated and we went back to the basics, nourishing food with as little processing as possible. My family did not come and thank me for the wonderful nutritious diet I was providing for them. Oh no, they far preferred the junk. It will be the same with the Church. There will be a lot of complaining and arguing as we go back to the basic Word of God.

"Yes, Lord," she said, "but even the dogs eat the crumbs that fall from their masters' table."

God is a merciful God. He has provided a way for the sinner to come back to Him. There is salvation and healing and abundance enough for every man, woman and child in the world. When we eat the true bread of heaven, crumbs will fall and the hurting can receive healing and deliverance, even when they are not Christians. However, to receive the bounty of God's blessings you must have the bread of Heaven, Jesus.

As we eat the true bread, it becomes our body, or we become His Body. Our cells are actually constructed from the food we ingest. We then are able to go out and minister to the masses that need Him with power.

Then Jesus answered, "Woman, you have great faith! Your request is granted." And her daughter was healed from that very hour.

It is faith in the complete Word of God that will grant our requests. Jesus meets this woman's needs even though she was not part of His mission, because God loves us all. From the hour we return to faith in Almighty God, and realize He has not changed His plan, we will be healed.

The provision of God's salvation plan for the world will be implemented, as the Church becomes the power that God intends it to be. When we stand up and take our rightful position as children of God, and use that position to conquer the enemy, His kingdom will come.

As the nations see the power of God to set people free in these last days, they will come running to the Church. She will take in a mighty harvest as faith in God grows and is imparted to the watching world. Healing is for this very hour, this special time of the anointing of the Holy Spirit of God.

Believers

This miracle deliverance of a possessed boy is recorded in Mark 9:14-29.

A man in the crowd answered, "Teacher, I brought you my son, who is possessed by a spirit that has robbed him of speech.

The Church has been possessed by a spirit of unbelief which has robbed her of her speech. She has failed to use the power of prophecy, and failed to speak God's true Word. This spirit has gripped the Church with a death hold for hundreds of years.

It is Jesus, the teacher, who can set the Church free from this spirit who has robbed her of her ability to speak the Word.

Whenever it seizes him, it throws him to the ground. He foams at the mouth, gnashes his teeth and becomes rigid.

Nothing will throw your relationship with your heavenly Father to the ground faster than to deny the power of God's Word. Those leaders in the Church that have their doctrines questioned do exactly what is described here. They foam at the mouth and grind their teeth. The more you talk to them the more rigid they become. They are in bondage to a spirit that denies the true power and ability of God to perform what He has said. Even worse, when others find the power of God they come against them.

I asked your disciples to drive out the spirit, but they could not.

Even though there have been revivals and teachers that have come up in the past hundreds of years to deliver the Church from this spirit, they have not been able to overcome it. It still holds a grip on most congregations. There are few places that are moving in any kind of power, and nowhere that I know of that has the full power available to the Church in Acts.

"O unbelieving generation," Jesus replied, "how long shall I stay with you? How long shall I put up with you?

This is truly an unbelieving generation. The Holy Spirit has said to the churches that Jesus is coming back. He is coming soon, and He shall no longer tolerate the unbelief that has permeated the Church.

Bring the boy to me." So they brought him. When the spirit saw Jesus, it immediately threw the boy into convulsions.

The Church must be brought back to Jesus. The true Jesus is filled with miracle working power. He is the one that walked on the water and turned the water into wine. The same Jesus that raised the dead and healed the sick and set the prisoner free.

When the Church comes back to Him, and the signs and wonders increase, the old guard is going to go into convulsions. There will be many that will not accept the new wine and will leave. But I say, nothing will stop this last move of God upon the earth.

He fell to the ground and rolled around, foaming at the mouth.

Falling to the ground represents the falling back to the dust from which man was taken; it is a return to sin and mortality. The preachers will foam at the mouth as they attack the prophets that began to stand forth, but they will not succeed. Those that refuse this move will lose their pulpit, as many desert tradition and come to the healing Jesus.

Those that rise up will become the warriors to bring the kingdom of God to completion.

Jesus asked the boy's father, "How long has he been like this?" "From childhood," he answered. It has often thrown him into fire or water to kill him. But if You can do anything take pity on us and help us."

The Church has been in this state since the early days of its childhood. There has not been another power Church since the Church of Acts,. The spirit of unbelief was brought into the doctrines, and the power was extinguished.

God has attempted to remove this spirit of unbelief from His Church by throwing it into the fire and water of the Holy Spirit, but to no avail. Men steeped in tradition and blind to the truth have remained in control.

When we come back to God in repentance and plead to God to take this blindness and unbelief away from us, He will not fail to come.

"If You can?" Said Jesus. "Everything is possible for him who believes."

The words "if You can" are the root of the spirit of unbelief. The one who takes the ax to that root and understands that everything is possible for him who believes, will be ready for the mighty work of God.

Immediately the boy's father exclaimed, "I do believe, help me overcome my unbelief!"

141

We need to plead with God to take away any remaining unbelief in us. Understand that the Word of God is true, and it is as true today as it was the day it came from God's mouth. He is the same yesterday, today and forever. We shall overcome all of our circumstances when we overcome our unbelief.

When Jesus saw that a crowd was running to the scene, He rebuked the evil spirit.

Look out, here come the crowds. As Jesus rebukes this spirit and the Church again believes, there will be an outpouring of miracles and mighty acts of God. The churches that have rebuked this spirit will be overflowing. They will need to start training people to counsel and assist new believers, and equip the warriors. When the battle starts there will be little time before His return.

"You deaf and mute spirit," He said, "I command you come out of him and never enter him again."

Christ is about to open our ears to hear the Word, and loose our tongues to speak it. As He commands that spirit to go, it will never enter the Church again. The evidence of His power will be so overwhelming, there will be no choice to believe or leave.

The spirit shrieked, convulsed him violently and came out. The boy looked so much like a corpse that many said; "He's dead."

It is not going to be a pretty sight when the spirit of unbelief is stripped from the Church. There will be yelling and screaming, convulsing the people. A convulsion shakes the person having a seizure, and there is coming a mighty shaking of God's holy Church. Many will say the Church has not survived, it is dead.

But Jesus took him by the hand and lifted him to his feet, and he stood up.

Jesus will take us by the hand and lift us up. We will stand up again, a mighty army of the saints of God, arrayed for battle.

After Jesus had gone indoors, His disciples asked Him privately, "Why couldn't we drive it out?"

The leaders of the Church have not been able to cast out this spirit of unbelief because they have partaken of it. You cannot drive out of someone else what you harbor in yourself. Jesus told us that you must remove the beam from your eye before you can see to take the speck out of someone else's eye.

He replied, "This kind can come out only by prayer."

Getting on our faces before God in repentance is the only way this spirit can be cast out of the Church. Many have been taught since infancy that the miracles had ceased with the apostles of Acts. Many have had their questions answered by theological rationalizations that prevented the seed of belief in the miracles from rooting.

It is time to repent of our unbelief. Get on your knees and ask God to reveal the truth to your heart. Do not put more faith in what man has told you than you do in the Word of God. There are multitudes of people in desperate need of the power of God, and He only works on this earth through believers. If you do not believe, you will not have the promise.

Receive Your Sight

This miracle healing of a blind man on the road to Jericho is recorded in Luke 18:35-43.

As Jesus approached Jericho, a blind man was sitting by the roadside begging.

144

Jesus is approaching the place where the walls fell down with a shout! The walls of unbelief and doubt are about to come down. We have had the beginnings of the move of God for this age. The priests and army of God have begun marching around the Church and are ready to sound the battle cry.

The Church has been sitting and begging for a true move of God to eliminate her problems. Nothing has worked and she is blind.

When he heard the crowd going by, he asked what was happening.

The crowd is beginning to gather and pass by the dead, quiet churches. As people see the move of God they will ask what is going on. People are being healed, there is power manifesting in our midst, and as it increases multitudes will be asking, "What is happening?"

They told him, "Jesus of Nazareth is passing by."

Jesus is passing by the dead Church. As the Spirit begins to move, more and more will walk in an anointing that has not been seen for thousands of years.

He called out, "Jesus, Son of David, have mercy on me!"

There are believers that are beginning to call out to the King of Kings for mercy. We must call out to Jesus, our King. Recognize that He came to have mercy on all of us for all of our problems. Sickness was included in the redemption. The prosperity plan of God is waiting to be implemented. Sin will go when we yield to Him.

Those who led the way rebuked him and told him to be quiet, but he shouted all the more, "Son of David, have mercy on me!"

The leaders of the Church have tried to still the voice of God coming through the Full Gospel movement. They have come against this movement, rebuked it, and tried to quiet it.

It is time the people shouted to bring that wall down. The wall of unbelief in the full Word of God must go. We need mercy from our King.

Jesus stopped and ordered the man to be brought to Him. When he came near, Jesus asked him, "What do you want Me to do for you?"

Jesus will stop passing the Church by when she calls to Him. He will order her to be brought before

146

Him, and ask what she wants. Whatever she needs, He is there to meet that need through faith.

"Lord, I want to see."

We must realize we are blind before we are willing to get our vision checked. We have to want to see before God can move. It is imperative that you know you have a problem, and what that problem is, before you can solve it.

There are areas of our lives filled with prejudices of which we must become aware. Racial tensions, denominational differences, generation gaps, feminist issues – the list goes on. We are called to love every person on the face of the planet. The blindness engulfs us all.

Jesus said to him, "Receive your sight; your faith has healed you."

As we take our blindness to Jesus, we will receive our sight. It is faith in a living Christ that will set us free. We must realize He is the answer to every problem. Spiritual blindness can only be healed by the revelation of the Holy Spirit to define the problem, and then remove it.

Immediately he received his sight and followed Jesus, praising God. When all of the people saw it, they also praised God.

We shall rejoice as we bring in the harvest. When our sight has been restored, we shall follow Jesus and see mighty signs and wonders. Every person shall see, and they too shall praise God. The mighty move of God will come with such signs and wonders every man will take notice. They will be forced to take sides, to believe or reject God's Son and His perfect plan.

Be Opened

This miracle healing of a deaf-mute man is recorded in the gospel of Luke 7:32–35.

There some people brought to Him a man who was deaf and could hardly talk, and they begged Him to place His hand on the man.

Those that are beginning to feel the power of God in their lives will begin to bring in the deaf Church that is hardly able to speak the truth. They will plead with Jesus to place His hand on their brothers and sisters in Christ.

After He took Him aside, away from the crowd, Jesus put His fingers into the man's ears.

To be healed of this deafness, you must come to Jesus alone, away from following the crowd, and have the Savior put His hand upon you.

The Word says in Romans 10:17, "So then faith comes by hearing, and hearing by the Word of God." (KJV) Although the normal interpretation of this verse is we get faith by hearing the Word of God, that is not what it says. It says, faith comes by hearing, and hearing comes by the Word of God. In other words, through hearing the Word of God the "ears of our hearts" are opened, and then we receive faith. Until Christ opens the ears of our hearts, we do not understand the Word, and we have no faith to apply it.

The Church needs the hand of Jesus to open the ears of her heart so she can then speak the truth plainly.

Then He spit and touched the man's tongue.

It says in Revelation 3:16, "So, because you are lukewarm – neither hot nor cold – I am about to spit you out of My mouth." The Lord wants a hot Church, on fire and speaking His Word. He will touch the tongue of those who submit to Him and whose ears He has opened, and they shall speak His words. The rest He shall spit out.

He looked up to heaven and with a deep sigh said to him, "Ephphatha!" (which means, "Be opened!").

We are to look up to heaven and weep before our God for Him to open our eyes and our ears and our mouths. We were created to worship Him and bring forth His glory on this planet. To do this we must go to Him in great repentance and seek His face until the fire falls.

Be open to God. Return to Him with a heart filled with yearning for His will in your life. Seek Him while He may be found, for soon there will be night and it will be too late.

At this, the man's ears were opened, his tongue was loosed and he began to speak plainly.

The Gospel of Jesus is a simple word. There are not any great theological implications that would keep even a child from serving Him. When our ears are opened to the truth, we will speak plainly. There is no need for long discourses or mumbo jumbo. Just yield to God and follow the Word He has provided. Love one another. Forgive your enemies. Eliminate sin, which is hurting others. Love God. Believe what He told you in His Word.

We have a new believer in our congregation with whom Gene and I have been working. She has no church background and does not know the Bible well. We have taught her to use the Concordance in her Bible to look up verses that apply to her life.

Recently she had some problems at work and said she was having trouble submitting to authority. Without saying anything, Gene reached for his Bible to look up the word "authority," and she grinned. "I already looked it up," she told him. She is learning to use the Word to solve her problems. This will open the ears of her heart to hear God's plan for her life. Notice that if you add one letter to the word "hear" you get "heart." What you hear goes into your heart.

You must be careful to hear good teaching that builds faith, or your belief system will be destroyed and you will not understand why the Word is not working in your life.

• The Message in the Miracles of Christ •

Chapter Seven

Take Authority

The teachers of the law have taken over the pulpits and seminary positions, and have taught a formula of obedience to rules and regulations rather than the relationship to the Heavenly Father that Jesus taught.

The following passage of another demon-possessed man is taken from Mark 1:21-28.

They went to Capernaum, and when the Sabbath came, Jesus went into the synagogue and began to teach.

Jesus is beginning to teach in His Church again. Those that fill the pulpits of the earth in His Name will get a revelation of the true Word of Christ. They will start to teach the complete Word that was taught by the Nazarene.

The people were amazed at His teaching, because He taught them as one who had authority, not as the teachers of the law.

There is an authority in God's Word that has not been spoken in the typical church. The teachers of the law have taken over the pulpits and seminary positions, and have taught a formula of obedience to rules and regulations rather than the relationship to the Heavenly Father that Jesus taught. When we go back to the Scriptures we see that Jesus gave us authority to use His Name and be overcomers. To do that we must have authority.

Just then a man in their synagogue who was possessed by an evil spirit cried out, "What do you want with us, Jesus of Nazareth."

An evil spirit of belief in another power grips the Church. Whenever we fail to take our authority, satan will take it from us, just as he did in the Garden.

156

What Jesus wants is for us to rise up and take the dominion He handed us when He went back to Heaven. In Matthew 28:18 He told His disciples, "All authority in heaven and on earth has been given to Me. Therefore go and make disciples of all nations, baptizing them in the name of the Father and of the Son and of the Holy Spirit, and teaching them to obey everything I have commanded you." Jesus said all authority had been given to Him and He turned around and used it to empower His disciples.

In Mark 16: 17 & 18, we read that after He commanded them, He named the signs that would follow them. "And these signs will accompany those who believe: In my Name they will drive out demons; they will speak in new tongues; they will pick up snakes with their hands; and when they drink deadly poison, it will not hurt them at all; they will place their hands on sick people they will recover." Jesus equipped us for a mission and then gave signs that the mission is being accomplished. Look behind you. If these signs are not following you and me, there is something wrong.

Much of the problem is that if the power is not flowing and signs and wonders are not occurring, the Church blames God, or the people say, "I tried it and it doesn't work." If it is not working there is something wrong with YOU, not God. He does not change, so what has changed? It is either you are not believing, or not obeying, or not following His Word in some way. Start looking for the problem in yourself, and God will show you what it is. Then you can correct it and will do what you have been commanded to do.

Have you come to destroy us? I know who you are – the Holy One of God.

Jesus has indeed come to destroy the works of satan and his demons. They know who He is. Isn't it interesting that the religious people had no clue as to His true identity, but the demons knew Him? We must remember He left us to clean up the earth and return dominion to Him. In I Corinthians 15:24 it says, "For He must reign until He has put all His enemies under His feet." We are His Body, and feet are on the Body not the head. The enemy needs to be under our feet. We shall crush satan's head (authority), and replace that head (authority) with Christ's.

"Be quiet," said Jesus sternly. "Come out of him."

Jesus is commanding the voice of doubt and unbelief to be quiet and come out of His Church. He has said we shall be free of the influence of evil. We are to be under His head, and only His head.

The evil spirit shook the man violently and came out of him with a shriek.

The Church shall shake as the authority of the Word of God replaces tradition and doubt. There's going to be some screaming and crying. Many will fight this move of God, but He will take back control of His Body.

The people were all so amazed that they asked each other, "What is this? A new teaching – and with authority! He even gives orders to evil spirits and they obey Him."

A new teaching with authority will replace all of the dogma and division in His Body. He will take back control through the power of His Word and the miracles that come forth. Multitudes will see an answer in Jesus that has been disguised by the teachings they have heard all of their lives. They shall come running to the Almighty God, and He shall set them free.

He will command the evil spirits to leave through the voice of the Church.

News about Him spread quickly over the whole region of Galilee.

News will spread quickly with the global communication network now in place. The media will begin to cover events, and soon worldwide revival will sweep out of control. The traditional churches that have lost the truth will change or die. Those that have never known the Gospel will flock in. A fire is about to be lit that will change the very face of the globe.

Clear Your Vision

The following miracle of another blind man is found only in Mark 8:22-26.

They came to Bethsaida, and some people brought a blind man and begged Jesus to touch him.

The name of the town Bethsaida means "place of nets." It is the time and place to begin preparing the nets for the final harvest for the Church.

Some people brought a blind man to Jesus, begging Him to touch him. The blind Church is begging for a touch from the Master, for she cannot complete her mission in her present state.

He took the blind man by the hand and led him outside the village.

He will take the Church by the hand and lead her to a place of healing. It must be outside of the place she is living, outside of the place where she has stayed for the past millenniums.

When He had spit on the man's eyes and put His hands on him, Jesus asked, "Do you see anything?" He looked up and said, "I see people; they look like trees walking around."

The Church looks up to God, and she begins to see. This is the present state of the Church, for there is a faith movement within the Body of Christ, which is beginning to see the truth of God's Word.

She sees the people, but they do not yet look like God's anointed Church. They look like the tree of knowledge of good and evil is still evident in their lives.

Once more Jesus put His hands on the man's eyes. Then his eyes were opened, his sight was restored, and he saw everything clearly.

Jesus again puts His hands on the Church with a stronger anointing, and her sight is restored. At that point she will see everything clearly, and she will be able to function in the capacity for which she was created.

Jesus sent him home, saying, "Don't go into the village."

Once the Church is healed and seeing clearly, she must not go back to the place she was living before. She cannot abide in sin and defeat and see. It is time for a new place where the Holy Spirit of God dwells. She needs to move from the tabernacle to the temple of God's glory, and place the mercy seat in her heart.

Each new revelation of God has unveiled a higher calling for man. The call and walk of Abraham was not as high as that of Moses, nor was Moses' walk as high as the walk of Jesus. Each calling brings us to a new dimension of a relationship with God.

The Church has dwelt very comfortably with the concept of John's baptism and a doctrine of repentance, but she has failed to take in the full measure of the redemption. The Holy Spirit is necessary for the Church to walk in power, for He said we would be better after He left, for then we would have the Spirit.

Living in the Spirit is also higher than just speaking in tongues. It is the living, breathing power of God in us, and He enables us to do the exploits of God Almighty through our earthly flesh. What a glorious calling He has given us!

Straighten Up!

Luke is the only Gospel that records the miracle of the crippled woman in the synagogue. It is found in the 13th chapter, verses 10–16.

On a Sabbath Jesus was teaching in one of the synagogues and a woman was there who had been crippled by a spirit for eighteen years.

Jesus is teaching in the Church again, and the Church has been crippled with a spirit for 1,800 years. Ever since the Church of Acts faded into the powerless structure we see today, an evil spirit of belief in the power of satan has crippled the Church. Satan has power of darkness, but he was defeated completely by Jesus.

She was bent over and could not straighten up at all.

When confronted by an unruly child we often use the phrase "straighten up." The beautiful Bride of Christ is bent over and cannot straighten up. A person who is bent over can only look at the ground, rather than turn her eyes to Heaven. She sees the dust where satan dwells instead of the sun. What a perfect picture of the Church, bent over to see the ground rather than keep her eyes on the Son.

This woman had also lost her flexibility. She was unable to bend and move. The Church has become inflexible in many areas. Denominations have become dogmatic and exclusive in their doctrines. It is essential that the Body of Christ be able to move with the Spirit of God. We must be flexible in the areas of unessential issues.

When Jesus saw her, He called her forward and said to her, "Woman you are set free from your infirmity."

Christ has come to His Church in the last day to straighten her up. He will call her to move forward, and receive healing. Jesus wants His Bride to be free to come to Him when He calls.

Then He put His hands on her, and immediately she straightened up and praised God.

When Jesus places His hands on the Church in the power of the coming restoration, she will straighten up, and she will lift her hands in praise to God. The Lord inhabits the praises of His people, and as the Church comes forth with praises on her lips, she will be able to look up and see the King.

She will be loose, able to move in the Spirit to do the works of Christ upon the earth.

Indignant because Jesus had healed on the Sabbath, the synagogue ruler said to the people, "There are six days for work. So come and be healed on those days, not on the Sabbath

There are only six days for work. God has given us 6,000 years to take back what satan stole, and complete the restoration of dominion to His people. Those days are over, and we have entered the Sabbath when no man shall work. We are in a small window of time between the end of the 6,000 years and the Rapture of the Church. This is the time of the Harvest – the great move of God. When the end comes like a flood, it will be a time of wrath

165

and judgment, not healing. We must come to Him NOW while there is still time.

The Lord answered him, "You hypocrites! Doesn't each of you on the Sabbath untie his ox or donkey from the stall and lead it out to give it water?

The Lord will eliminate the hypocrites in the coming hour. The wheat and the tares will be separated. Even in His rest God takes care of what belongs to Him. He is taking those that are His and leading them to the water of the Holy Spirit.

Then should not this woman, a daughter of Abraham, whom satan has kept bound for eighteen long years, be set free on the Sabbath day from what bound her?"

The Church is a daughter of Abraham, and all of the covenant promises belong to her (see Gal. 3:29). In spite of the resistance of the Church leaders, Christ is going to set His Church free for the Sabbath rest that is to come. A rapture will remove her from the coming wrath, but first the Church must come into the perfection of the Bride.

Satan has been ahead for 1,800 years, but the tide is turning. Christ is loosing His people for a final battle, and they will win. All that has bound her will be removed, and she shall receive power from on High. The mighty army of God is beginning to come together for the last battle. God has known the end from the beginning, and those that choose to wear His uniform will live forever in glory.

Let the River Flow

The healing of the man with dropsy is found in Luke 14:1-6.

One Sabbath, when Jesus went to eat in the house of a prominent Pharisee, He was being carefully watched.

The Church is watching the new movement of God that is beginning to flow. The prominent denominational leaders are eating with Jesus; they share communion with Him, but they are watching to catch Him in something that goes against their theology.

There in front of Him was a man suffering from dropsy.

Dropsy is a disease that causes a person to retain water and swell. It is caused by failure of the kidneys to remove the impurities in a person's body.

Failure to eliminate sin will cause impurity in the body, and at that point the Holy Spirit will not be able to flow. Some of the Church is being filled with the Holy Spirit, but it never flows out of them. They stagnate where they are because they do not release the Spirit to heal and manifest in miracles.

If the heart is not sound and healthy, the kidneys will fail and the water will be retained in the body. We must have a pure and holy heart, right with God, beating in unison with His.

When the Spirit does not flow like a river, it fails to accomplish God's mission in that person. The Spirit of God always has a ministry for each Christian. Those that are filled with the Holy Spirit at salvation are invited to move on in growth, continually being filled and then touching others with the power of God.

There are many levels of that river. What starts as a trickle, can become a creek and then a raging torrent as the Spirit cleanses the vessel. But, you can dam the Spirit by failing to remove the impurities from your life. Water that is prevented from flowing becomes polluted. If the Spirit in you is not flowing, your mission will never be accomplished.

Jesus asked the Pharisees and experts in the law, "Is it lawful to heal on the Sabbath or not?"

Those that live by the law will die by the law. Healing was central to Jesus' ministry while He was here on earth. It may not have been lawful to heal on the Sabbath, but Jesus said He was greater than the Sabbath. The Church has failed to continue in Her healing ministry, and thus she has not fulfilled her mission.

But they remained silent.

Pride fills the legalist, and they refuse to acknowledge their sin. It is essential to speak the truth of God, and allow it to manifest within the Church, or Christ is not ruling. We must speak God's Word and answer His questions.

So taking hold of the man, He healed him and sent him away.

Christ will take hold of the Church and heal her to finish the work He started. He will send her to the Four Corners of the globe in the coming time, and she shall be triumphant.

Then He asked them, "If one of you has a son or an ox that falls into a well on the

Sabbath day, will you not immediately pull him out?"

When we have a child or an animal that is in trouble we immediately rush to help. Do you remember the little girl that fell into a well a few years back, and the stir it caused across the Nation? How much more should we be concerned about those that come each Sunday to hear God's Word, and go home empty. The pit of Hell into which they are about to fall is terrifying. It is time to stand up and preach the truth, the whole truth and nothing but the truth.

The leaders must pull out the Bible and begin to teach the unadulterated Word of God. Signs and Wonders will flow as the move of God begins. The denominational churches will receive a tremendous anointing of the Holy Spirit, and the miracles will astound everyone.

And they had nothing to say.

There is much to say on the side of the Gospel, and God is looking for those with the courage to say it to a dying world. The Word must come through the lips of the Church for God to work. He has given dominion to man, and it must be through man that victory is won. If God were to take the dominion back that He gave to man in the Garden of Eden, it would be stealing. God honors His commitments even though man has failed to honor his own.

Praise the Lord

The miracle healing of ten men with leprosy is recorded in Luke:17:11-19.

Now on His way to Jerusalem, Jesus traveled along the border between Samaria and Galilee.

Jesus is on His way to Jerusalem again. Two thousand years ago He went to be crucified, this time He is going to take over. He has traveled between the Jews, to whom He was sent, and the Gentiles, those outside of the Jewish system.

As He was going into a village ten men who had leprosy met Him.

Leprosy was a disease that was used as an analogy for sin in the Scriptures. These men represent the sin filled denominations of the present day Church. The numeral ten represents responsibility.

These denominations and the religious leaders are about to meet Jesus, the risen Master.

171

*They stood at a distance and called out in
a loud voice, "Jesus, Master, have pity on
us!"*

These men have taken responsibility for their
condition. They have taken a good look at
themselves and realize they are in a sinful state.
They are standing at a distance; Jesus is sitting
next to His Father, and they are calling out for
mercy.

*When He saw them, He said, "Go, show
yourselves to the priests."*

He just tells them to go to the Church and show
themselves to the leaders. Those that realize their
sinfulness must begin to show their leaders the
state they are in. They must know they are in
trouble before they are willing to call 911.

It is easy to see that these men certainly knew
they were sick. They were outcasts and not allowed
to go into society, but I say that most church
members are hiding the sin in their hearts from all
the people they know. They live a secret life, and it
is time to confess. It is in going to the high priest,
Jesus, that we may confess and be forgiven.

And as they went, they were cleansed.

When we go to repent, we will be cleansed. It is a necessary step to the coming restoration.

One of them, when he saw he was healed came back, praising God in a loud voice.

One man out of ten comes back to Jesus to praise God. How many are saved, delivered and started on a new life, and yet fail to give praise. The restoration will not take place until the Church learns to praise.

He threw himself at Jesus feet and thanked Him – and he was a Samaritan.

The Church must throw herself at the feet of Jesus with a heart over-flowing with thanksgiving. It is the foreigner, the Samaritan, that comes back – not the strong church member. How we need a breakthrough in true thanksgiving and praise in our churches.

The numeral one, the one that comes back, stands for the source, the beginning; and the one that comes to praise and give thanks will begin the restoration of the Church.

Jesus asked, "Were not all ten cleansed? Where are the other nine? Was no one found to return and give praise to God except this foreigner?"

Nine is the last single digit and stands for judgment. God will come soon and pass judgment on every man. Those who fail to praise God and thank Him will be cast out with the unbelievers.

We need more than just cleansing; we need Holiness. There is a call to a higher life than the Church has preached. There is a need for those that will be committed to worship and praise God and follow His voice.

Then He said to him, "Rise and go, your faith has made you well."

It is faith that has made this man well. He came and confessed his need, repented, and then came back to praise God and thank Him. At that point he has faith, and he is well. This man left with a changed life. Not only was he healed, but also he had a new commitment and understanding of God.

I am sure the other nine were healed. The question is, did they keep it? Salvation is not the goal; it is the beginning of the process. We need to get people saved, but then we must disciple them and teach them to praise God and thank Him. After they learn the Word and grow in grace, they are able to go out and replicate themselves and bring more into the Body.

• Take Authority •

Chapter Eight

• The Message in the Miracles of Christ •

No More of This

Those that are steeped in tradition cannot comprehend something that does not exist in their own theology.

The miracle of healing the servant of the High Priest when they went to arrest Jesus is found in Luke 22:50–51.

When Jesus' followers saw what was going to happen, they said, "Lord, should we strike with our swords?"

When there are attacks on Jesus and the Church it is our instinct to reach out with our weapons and fight back. The disciples saw them

179

come to take away their beloved Jesus, and they struck out at them.

Persecution is coming to the Church, and you notice it is coming from the religious people, not the Romans. It is always the legalists that come to arrest each new move of God. Those that are steeped in tradition cannot comprehend something that does not exist in their own theology.

And one of them struck the servant of the high priest, cutting off his right ear.

Peter is identified as the person wielding the sword in John 18:26. He was the leader of the disciples, and this message is to the leaders of the Last Day Church. The Church has reached out against her own body with a sword, and cut off her ear, or the ability to hear God's true Word.

But Jesus answered, "No more of this!" And He touched the man's ear and healed him.

Jesus is commanding the full truth again be preached. He is also giving the command to quit attacking those of the Body we don't agree with. As long as a practice is in accordance to Scriptural principles, we are forbidden to come against the person that believes it.

My brother-in-law, who is now home with the Lord, used to frequently get in theological discussions with me when we were young. At the time we both attended evangelical denominational churches, but I was constantly seeking the truth of the Scripture. We had a lengthy debate about tongues, which I did not speak at the time, nor had I ever attended a church that taught the practice of speaking in tongues. I can remember vehemently upholding the practice because God's Word stated it should not be forbidden.

It was years later, after reading *Good Morning Holy Spirit* by Benny Hinn, that I received that gift. At the time I argued with my brother-in-law I knew I loved the Lord, and served Him, but I also knew that there was more out there, and I hungered for it. I still do; I want it all, every possible drop of God available.

When we come to Jesus and let Him direct our ways, we will stop attacking our own Body, and uphold it. There will be a great healing among the denominational churches in the coming days. God wants one family, united in love for each other. That is the sign by which the world will know we belong to Him.

Resurrecting the Body

John 4: 46-53 is the only record of the miracle of healing the royal official's son.

Once more He visited Cana in Galilee, where He had turned the water into wine.

Jesus is returning to the place where miracles began for His Last Days Church. The power of the Lord will again rise up in His Body.

And there was a certain royal official whose son lay sick at Capernaum.

Capernaum was His home after leaving Galilee for His ministry, and many miracles took place there. The Church today is sick because the miracle power of the Holy Spirit has been missing. We need to go home; back to Capernaum.

When this man heard that Jesus had arrived in Galilee from Judea, he went to Him and begged Him to come and heal his son, who was close to death.

We came from a denominational background and have only been attending a Full Gospel church for about two years. I was filled with the Spirit before that, but we could not find a church we were both comfortable in. We have fallen in love with the enthusiasm and joy in the Charismatic congregations we have been a part of here and in Arkansas. Occasionally there is a church service on TBN that has the old type of worship we endured for so many years. We call it the "dead church," and I cannot even abide watching it.

My husband Gene was filled with the Spirit, and he has been blessed with a powerful anointing. He hasn't quite gotten used to my dancing yet, and I won't tell you what my children have said, but I wouldn't go back for anything the earth has to offer.

We need to cry out for those congregations that are "dead" and plead with the Lord to come. The Church is close to death because of the failure to understand the supernatural. The onslaught of humanism and scientific confrontation has devastated the basic belief in an Almighty Creator who interacts with His people, and sometimes reaches down to supercede natural law.

"Unless you people see miraculous signs and wonders," Jesus told him, "You will never believe."

It is absolutely true that the Church today needs to see signs and wonders to bring back to life the belief in miracles. God is about to show the world

His power, and it will cause a great out pouring of souls for the final harvest.

The royal official said, "Sir, come down before my child dies."

Prayer is the petition of the Body of believers to the Father, and we need a wave of fervent prayer for the Revival of the Church. As Royal officials of the Church of God, we need to petition our King of Kings to come with power.

We need Jesus to come down, to intervene before the Church dies. God has said the gates of Hell will not prevail, and He is about to come with great signs and wonders, such as the world has not seen since Jesus walked the earth. Like the dry bones in Ezekiel's vision, the Church shall live and breathe the Spirit again, but He will only come when He is invited.

Jesus replied, "You may go. Your son will live."

This Church, this Body of believers may go forth, for God's Son shall live in her. God's Church will not die; it will rise up and become the power God sent His Son to procure. There will be a mighty, glorious Church that Jesus shall return to claim.

The man took Jesus at His word and departed. While he was still on the way, his servants met him with the news that his boy was living.

The time is short before His return. Let us take Jesus at His Word and get busy. While we are on the way, for He is the Way, the servants of God will bring the news that Jesus is alive and well in His Body.

When he inquired as to the time when his son got better, they said to him, "The fever left him yesterday at the seventh hour."

Jesus will bring to life this almost dead Body in the perfect time of the Father. The seventh hour is the hour of perfection. The fever of activities and programs is leaving and the Body is beginning to revive.

Then the father realized that this was the exact time at which Jesus had said to him, "Your son will live." So he and all his household believed.

As Jesus declares His Living Word for the Church, she shall live. As we speak forth His words from our pulpits with love and enthusiasm, the congregations will wake up and believe in the most Holy Son of God and the completeness of His Word.

The Church shall return to prayer and praise, gathering together in meetings that seem to never end because of the reluctance of the people to leave the presence of God. We had an evangelist at our church a couple of weeks ago that stayed until 3 AM. We were not in a hurry to leave, but rather rejoiced in the mighty power of God in that place.

How different it was than the church we used to attend where we could set our clocks by when the service would begin and end. Exactly one hour, it never varied. Of course, they never had an encounter with the Holy Spirit who is eternal and fails to keep man's appointed times, only God's.

There is a promise in here for us that all of our households will believe. There will be a place for every child of every believer in these last days. The hearts of the children shall turn to their fathers.

When the Water is Stirred

The miracle of the invalid at the pool of Bethesda is recorded in John 5:1-9.

Some time later, Jesus went up to Jerusalem for a feast of the Jews.

Jesus is entering the city of Peace for a feast.

Now there is in Jerusalem near the Sheep Gate a pool, which in Aramaic is called Bethesda and which is surrounded by five covered colonnades.

Jesus said in John 10:9, "I am the gate; whoever enters through Me will be saved." This gate was the gate for the Sheep. We are the sheep. The name Bethesda means "house of mercy" in Hebrew. It is Jesus, the gate to the Father, who in mercy comes to His people.

The numeral five is symbolic of grace, and the five covered colonnades are symbolic of the five offices in the Church: Apostle, Prophet, Pastor, Teacher and Evangelist. The covering is the anointing of the Holy Spirit upon their ministry.

Here a great number of disabled people used to lie – the blind, the lame, and the paralyzed.

There are many people that come to the church service on Sunday and gather round the water, but never get in. They are the blind, the lame, the paralyzed, the deaf, the mute – a great number of disabled people.

One who was there had been an invalid for thirty-eight years.

This guy had been "attending services" for a long time. Thirty stands for maturity, time to step into the ministry God has given you, and eight for the beginning of a new order of things or regeneration. The ailing Church needs to grow into maturity and come to the Lord for healing and deliverance.

When Jesus saw him lying there and learned that he had been in this condition for a long time, He asked him, "Do you want to get well?"

Jesus sees us sitting there Sunday after Sunday and yet staying in the condition we were when we came. The Jews used to go in one door of the temple and out another to represent they were not the same after they worshiped God. We need to change as we attend services, to leave a different person than when we arrived.

Jesus is asking the Church, "Do you want to get well?"

"Sir," the invalid replied, "I have no one to help me into the pool when the water is stirred. While I am trying to get in, someone else goes down ahead of me."

He had laid there all of those years waiting and watching as others jumped in the water before he did. He had no one to help him, and the Church certainly needs help. They may be trying to get in, but unable to get up and move to the water of the Spirit because they are just plain too sick.

This man was faithful though, he came out no matter what was happening and waited for the angel to come. He should have been looking to Jesus instead of a building. Build a rrelationship with the risen Lord.

Then Jesus said to him, "Get up! Pick up your mat and walk."

Jesus is about to tell His Body to get up, pick up the mat it has been laying on, and walk. The Church has work to do, and it is time to get busy.

At once the man was cured, he picked up his mat and walked.

When He speaks with power in the coming anointing, those that have been faithfully waiting for Him will jump up, healed! The Body of Christ is about to have a mighty restoration of her power and she will be whole again.

The day on which this took place was a Sabbath, and so the Jews said to the man who had been healed, "It is the Sabbath; the law forbids you to carry your mat."

Of course, those that spout the law will come against the new move of God that is about to hit the Church. They will say the law forbids the miracles, it forbids the signs and wonders, and we cannot carry the anointing to a crippled, hurting world.

But he replied, "The man who made me well said to me, "Pick up your mat and walk."

The One that has made us well will tell us what to do, and we must obey. It is time to get the Word of the Master straight and do His work. Many will not like the message or the messenger, but we must follow the voice of the Master.

So they asked him, "Who is this fellow who told you to pick it up and walk?"

They still don't recognize Jesus, even though it was His power that had done so much for them. The Church has failed to recognize her Lord when He appears.

The man who was healed had no idea who it was, for Jesus had slipped away into the crowd that was there.

In the crowd that will come into the Church with a flood in the last days, many will not know who Jesus really is. They will know they are healed and they will know they are free, but they will have to be taught the Scriptures and the truth of the Living Word of God.

We need to prepare to teach those that are about to flood the Church with their needs. Train the lay people and the clergy to respond to the harvest that will come in during this last hour of the last day.

Every church needs to start a program of discipleship for the new believers and obtain materials to instruct new members in the faith. I am not talking about doctrine, I am talking about basic teaching of Scripture. Just as our schools need to return to the basic teaching of the 3 Rs, the Church needs to return to the basic tenants of the faith.

> Later Jesus found him at the temple and said to him, "See, you are well again. Stop sinning or something worse may happen to you."

We must teach the Church to refrain from sin. To be healed and then remain in sin is not building God's kingdom on earth. We must teach the people to be holy and set apart. Those that know the truth will have a higher judgment. We must learn to eliminate sin on every level of our lives.

The man went away and told the Jews that it was Jesus who had made him well.

It is our place as a Church Body at this point in time to tell the Jews that Jesus is the Messiah they have longed for. I believe that there will be a working of the Holy Spirit upon the Jewish nation to prepare them for the coming day of the Lord.

They failed the first time He came to recognize Him, but they will receive Him this time. There is to be a ministry of this Last Days Church to the Jewish nation that will prepare the way for the Second Coming of the Lord. Unless they understand the Scriptures they will not look for Him even after the Rapture. The final fulfillment of all things will be when the Jews say, "Blessed is He who comes in the name of the Lord."

Go and Wash

The miracle healing of another blind man is recorded in John 9:1-7.

As He went along, He saw a man blind from birth.

The Last Days Church has been blind since birth. Almost every denomination is over 100 years old. A generation in the Scriptures is only 40 years. A World Wide Revival has not occurred for over 94 years. The last real revival that actually impacted all society was in 1904. A revival will impact society for the good for 40 years and then those that were changed die off, and the new generation does not have the fire. For a wonderful book on the revival cycles read *A Cure for All Ills*, by Relfe.

His disciples asked Him, "Rabbi, who sinned, this man or His parents, that he was born blind?"

The pointing of fingers will not help to heal the Church. It doesn't matter who sinned, what matters is the man is blind. The Church is blind, she cannot see the truth.

"Neither this man nor his parents sinned," said Jesus, "but this happened so that the work of God might be displayed in his life."

Those that really are the Church are the sinless Body of Christ. There is no sin that is charged to their account, for they are under the blood. That does not mean every person that warms a pew on Sunday, or every person that calls himself a

Christian is sinless. What it means is there are those that truly have followed what they have been taught and are sincere followers of Christ and part of His Body, but are still blind.

The status of the Church in general is sad, but the work of God is about to be displayed in the Church. The blind are going to see.

As long as it is day, we must do the work of Him who sent Me. Night is coming, when no one can work.

The time left before the coming of Jesus Christ to pick up His Bride is short. We are supposed to be doing the work of the Father, and it is crucial that we get busy NOW! The dark night of the tribulation looms on the horizon, even as the glorious Church shines in her final hour.

It is still day, He has not yet come. We must travail in prayer for the Lord to open our eyes.

While I am in the world, I am the light of the world.

Jesus is the light, but a man born blind cannot see the light. We must have our eyes healed before we can see the Lord of Hosts who is about to come for us.

Having said this, He spit on the ground, made some mud with the saliva, and put it on the man's eyes.

God created man from the dust of the ground and Jesus uses this dust to create eyes for the man born blind. He will create a new vision within His Body from the dust that we are. He has taken that which the Father created and restored it to the original plan of God. We see with a clear focus the plan that God has for us when we come to Jesus for healing. He will form whatever it is within us that is missing until the final shining hour when He returns for His creation.

"Go," he told him, "wash in the Pool of Siloam." (This word means Sent.)

In John 20:21 Jesus said, "As the Father has sent me, I am sending you." He has told us to go, wash and be clean of the dust, and go out to a lost and dying world. His mission is our mission and we are to do what He did.

So the man went and washed, and came home seeing.

When we obey God's Word to us and wash ourselves, we will see. It is those that see that will come home to be with the Lord. He has said He is coming for a Church without spot or wrinkle.

His neighbors and those who had formerly seen him begging asked, "Isn't this the same man who used to sit and beg?" Some claimed that he was. Others said, "No, he only looks like him."

The world that has been watching the blind Church begging for people to come, begging for finances, begging for survival, will see the power Church and be astounded at what they are accomplishing. People will not recognize the Church in the days to come.

But he himself insisted, "I am the man."

This power Church will stand up and insist that it is the Church that Jesus intended it to be. A Church fully capable of meeting the needs of mankind in the here and now.

"How then were your eyes opened?" they demanded.

"How could this happen?" many will ask. What is going on in the Church that these mighty miracles are taking place?

He replied, "The man they call Jesus made some mud and put it on my eyes. He told me to go to Siloam and wash. So I went and washed, and then I could see.

Jesus has sent us to clean up our act, and when we obey Him, we will see.

"Where is this man?" they asked.

Many will begin seeking Jesus and will look to Him for the first time.

"I don't know," he said.

We need to know Him, and point the way to the Savior for those that will come in during this final harvest of God. There are multitudes of lost and dying people that will flock to the Church during this Last Day. We must know how to show the way and be bold in our witness.

• The Message in the Miracles of Christ •

Chapter Nine

Just Believe

The following miracle of the healing of Jairus' daughter is found in Mark 5:21-43.

When Jesus had again crossed over by boat to the other side of the lake a large crowd gathered around Him while He was by the lake.

Jesus has returned to this side of heaven for the preparation of His Church in these last days. He has begun to gather a crowd as many churches are feeling the touch of Revival and an increase in the presence of the Holy Spirit in their meetings.

*Then one of the synagogue rulers, named
Jairus came there. Seeing Jesus. He fell at
His feet and pleaded earnestly with Him,*

There are those church leaders, however, that
are presiding over hopelessly lifeless congregations.
The name Jairus means "enlightener" in Hebrew.
Those pastors and members that want to bring the
light into the dying Church will come to Jesus and
fall at His feet, pleading earnestly to Him in prayer.

*My little daughter is dying. Please come
and put your hands on her so that she will
be healed and live.*

So many leaders of the Church dearly love the
people and are carrying a great burden for their
flock. They are pleading in prayer for the Master to
come and lay His powerful hands on the Church to
bring healing to her, that she may live.

So Jesus went with him.

Jesus is waiting to come to us when we ask. The
Spirit is hovering over the Body of Christ, ready to
impart the power of God into this ailing Body. He
will come with us as we supplicate in fervent
prayer.

(At this point the Scripture is interrupted for the
healing of the woman with the issue of blood. You

202

will find that miracle in Chapter 9, and now we continue on with the healing of Jairus' daughter)

While Jesus was still speaking some men came from the house of Jairus, the synagogue ruler.

Jesus is on His way and is interrupted by another needy person. There seem to be many delays while He is on the way to answer our prayers. It almost seems as though the possibility for true Revival in this Church is over. There are men coming with bad news about the state of the world and the Church.

"Your daughter is dead," they said, "Why bother the teacher any more?"

The appearance of death is on many congregations. The people have become lifeless and cold to the teaching of the Word. There are many people that deny the basic tenants of the faith, and leave the services with no changes in their life style. Many have been hurt or offended and are not even attending church anymore. The blood has stopped flowing. The breath is gone.

Ignoring what they said, Jesus told the synagogue ruler, "Don't be afraid, just believe."

We must not allow fear to creep in. There are letters being circulated that say the Lord has passed over the Church in America for it is beyond redemption. Do not believe such an evil report. God has not deserted His beloved.

He did not let anyone follow Him except Peter, James and John the brother of James.

The strong leaders, full of faith, will follow Him. Those that cannot believe or walk in fear will be left behind for the beginning of the coming move of God.

When they came to the home of the synagogue ruler, Jesus saw a commotion with people crying and wailing loudly.

The tears of the people are falling over the lack of Revival in this dead Church. Prayer meetings are being birthed that are the beginnings of the mourning for the sins of the people that will bring Jesus on the scene. Intercessors are being moved into position to plead for the Body of Christ.

He went in and said to them, "Why all this commotion and wailing? The child is not dead but asleep."

204

Jesus is about to come in. He will come and declare this child has not died, but has simply fallen asleep. It may be a coma, but there is still life in this body.

But they laughed at Him.

There are many that are laughing at the things of the Spirit. They cannot understand the supernatural events taking place, and they are scoffing at the possibility that such things even exist. There are multitudes of born again; Bible totin' Christians that do not believe that the God that heals and delivers even exists in this day.

After He put them all out, He took the child's father and mother and the disciples who were with Him, and went in where the child was.

Those that laugh and ridicule are ready to be put out. The miracles that are about to happen will leave many shut out from this last move of God. Jesus will take the faithful that love Him and believe His Word, and they shall go into the inner room to watch this Church rise from the dead.

He took her by the hand and said to her, "Talitha kowm!" (which means, "Little girl, I say get up!").

Jesus will take her people by the hand and say to her, "Get up!" Get moving. The power will begin to flow and the miracles will follow those that believe.

Immediately the little girl stood up and walked around (she was 12 years old). At this they were completely astonished.

This is going to be a quick work. The time is at hand and there will be a mighty move of God such as has never been seen before. Multitudes will come in and the world will look on with astonishment as God moves in this final hour of completion for His work.

Twelve is the number of manifest sovereignty, or the perfect Divine government on this earth. It is time that the people of God come alive and rule the earth as God intended when He created man. Jesus died that we might be the men and women Adam and Eve were created to be. A people created to rule, under God, in perfect communion with Him.

He gave strict orders not to let anyone know about this, and told them to give her something to eat.

The government of God is between you and Him. He does not intend to publicize His ways to the crowd, He works with us on an individual basis. We can learn of the precepts in a corporate church setting, but the very personal work of the Holy Spirit in my life is a relationship between God and me, and no one else is allowed to intrude upon that communion.

Jesus instructs the leaders to feed the people. They need to eat of the Living Bread and feast upon the Word. The communion that we partake of in Christ becomes our body and blood as we become His body and blood. There is a unity with Christ and then with each other as we move into a deep relationship with God.

Don't Cry

Luke 7:11-15 tells of this miracle where Jesus raised the widow's son from the dead.

Soon afterward, Jesus went to a town called Nain, and His disciples and a large crowd went along with Him.

The name of the town, Nain, in Hebrew means a home or a habitation. Jesus has come home to abide with His people; to be the head of their Body. Many will come to new life in the Lord in the coming days.

As He approached the town gate, a dead person was being carried out – the only son of His mother, and she was a widow.

Jesus is the gate, the entrance for those that would go to abide with God Almighty. Coming forth from this gate is a son who has died, and his mother is mourning for him. The tears of the mothers are going up before God's throne over the sons and daughters that have come out from the Church and are seemingly lost in the world. They are dead to the teachings of their childhood and the preaching they sat under as a babe in their mother's arms.

And a large crowd from town was with her.

There are many that are crowding around this mother, whose son is lost to her. There seems to be lost children in almost every family in these days. Teens have been targeted by satan and his demons in so many areas. Drugs, alcohol, pornography, television, rock music, video games, free sex and many other temptations are facing our youth and many have died to their heritage.

I was babysitting for my two grandsons last week and they asked if they could watch a cartoon channel. I am not familiar with children's programming now, so I went in to check it out. It was a cartoon teaching them astrology, including what sign they were under. I was shocked at the blatant way satan has used the TV to teach his doctrines, while we are not allowed to pray in our children's schools. The forces of evil are using your own family room to program your children's mind through television.

When the Lord saw her, His heart went out to her and He said, "Don't cry."

As God is preparing to come back, He will begin a mighty work in the children of the faithful. We must claim the promise of God that He will save our children. His heart is going out to us over the tears of the mothers and fathers as they see their children lost in corruption and sin.

Then He went up and touched the coffin, and those carrying it stood still.

Those that are carrying off our youth are going to be stopped in their tracks. Jesus is about to touch the children of Christians in a powerful way. The revival that is coming is going to hit the campuses with great power, and there will be multitudes of young people turn to the Lord.

He said, "Young man, I say to you, get up!"

Jesus is about to speak His Word into our children. Those that have Christian moms and dads that have been faithful will come to Him. There will be a convicting power of the Holy Spirit that will move upon them in the Last Days.

The dead man sat up and began to talk, and Jesus gave him back to his mother.

These young people that have been dead to Christ shall sit up and begin to speak for Him again. The mothers will again receive their children back into the fold before the final harvest. Jesus is about to return our children to us, alive and well.

Loose Him

The following miracle of the raising of Lazarus from the dead is found in John 11:1-44.

Now a man named Lazarus was sick.

A man named Lazarus (which means God helped) was sick. In the original Greek the word man is implied by the use of the word "certain," which means any particular person or object. So, it really says "a person is sick."

The word for sick in the Greek means "to be feeble in any sense, diseased, impotent or weak."

The Christian of the typical church is impotent, unable to perform the miracles Christ commanded be performed. It is full of diseased people bound by the curse of sickness. It is full of weak ineffective people living their lives without the power of God to loose them from the bonds of satan.

He was from Bethany, the village of Mary and her sister Martha. This Mary, whose brother Lazarus now lay sick, was the same one who poured perfume on the Lord and wiped His feet with her hair.

Bethany means the "house of dates" in Hebrew. There is a date the Lord has made with His beloved Church. It is the town that contains the people Jesus loves with a great love, Mary, Martha and Lazarus. These people love the Lord and have ministered to Him in the beautiful act where Mary anointed Him with costly perfume and wiped His feet with her hair. They have the strongest relationship with the Lord that is recorded in Scripture, outside of His 12 disciples.

So the sisters sent word to Jesus, "Lord, the one you love is sick."

The sisters, which is often used as a synonym for Christian women, are calling on the Lord to let Him know the one that He loves is very sick. In

211

most churches the intercessors are women, and it is the women who are often the ones quietly loving and serving the Lord.

When He heard this, Jesus said, "This sickness will not end in death. No, it is for God's glory so that God's Son may be glorified through it."

The sickness of those that Jesus loves will not end in death. The disease that pervades His beloved Church will be used to bring great glory to God, and Jesus will be glorified through it.

Jesus loved Martha and her sister and Lazarus. Yet when He heard that Lazarus was sick, He stayed where He was two more days.

Jesus has loved His Church for the past ages, and even though He knew she was sick since the Church in Acts, and seemed to be unable to function in the revelation of victory, He stayed where He was in Heaven by the side of the Father.

Then He said to His disciples, "Let us go back to Judea."

When Jesus returns He is not coming to America or Rome or Argentina, He is coming back to Judea. The place where it began is where it will end. It was the job of the Church to take the gospel and preach it to every creature. His job was to enable us to do it. After we finish our job, He will come to reign with us from Jerusalem.

"But Rabbi," they said, "a short while ago the Jews tried to stone You, and yet You are going back there?"

The Jewish nation rejected Jesus and hung Him on the tree, and yet that is where He is returning. Why? Because of the covenant God made eons ago with a man called Abraham and his descendants. The power of that word has not been broken nor can it ever be erased. Not even the death of Jesus on the cross broke the word that God gave to Abraham nor changed one letter on those promises.

Jesus answered, "Are there not twelve hours of daylight? A man who walks by day will not stumble, for he sees by this world's light. It is when he walks by night that he stumbles, for he has no light."

Jesus is the light of the world. He shines out through His people. We must walk in Him if we are to accomplish the mission God has given us. We need the light to prevent us from stumbling over our traditions or own feet. We need the light to keep us on the path He has laid out for us.

It is still day, and we need to use the little time we have left to finish the job before the night of the tribulation begins. Then they will walk by night, for the light of Christ will have left this world with the Church in the Rapture.

After He had said this, He went on to tell them, "Our friend Lazarus has fallen asleep, but I am going there to wake him up."

Jesus then says the Church has been asleep, but He is coming to wake her up.

His disciples replied, "Lord, if he sleeps, he will get better."

Church leaders think they can institute a new program or sing a new song or try a new prayer and she will get better. They believe the sleep upon the Church is OK because it is not making any waves. Things are going on as they have been going on for several hundred years. "Everything is going to be all right," they think. "It is going to get better. Look how peaceful they are."

I remember the nightly ritual of checking the children before going to bed and watching them

214

sleep in their cribs. I always kissed them and told them I loved them and tucked them in one last time. Many pastors are doing exactly that as they watch their sleeping congregations, totally oblivious to the fact they need to be awake and alive.

Jesus had been speaking of his death, but His disciples thought He meant natural sleep.

The last enemy to be overcome is death. Jesus defeated satan on the cross. The serpent on the pole in the wilderness was representative of Christ. It was not Jesus who died on that cross, for He simply went to the tomb for a nap and then got up for a fight. It was satan's reign that ended, and after the Church mops up the effects of the disaster at Eden, death will be defeated forever.

So then He told them plainly, "Lazarus is dead, and for your sake I am glad I was not there, so that you may believe. But let us go to him."

The Church is dead, but it's rebirth will make believers of multitudes. Jesus is coming to His leaders and then going to the congregations. Then they will go to the highways and byways as the crowds see the power and glory of Christ in them.

Then Thomas (called Didymus) said to the rest of the disciples, "Let us also go, that we may die with Him."

Didymus means "the twin." Each one of us has a spirit, which is redeemed when we are saved, and the flesh that must die. We are twins. Thomas is saying we must die with Him. That is very true, we must die to ourselves to live in Him. We must understand Christ expects our all, and then He turns around and gives it back multiplied. When we die with Him in the flesh, we will live with Him, forever in the spirit.

On His arrival, Jesus found that Lazarus had already been in the tomb four days.

The four days Lazarus is in the tomb represents the four ages of the Church, during which death still reigned. The Church in Acts, the Roman Catholic Church, the Protestant Church and the Last Days Church. We are in the era of the Last Days Church and it is about to be resurrected from the dead.

Bethany was less than two miles from Jerusalem, and many Jews had come to Martha and Mary to comfort them in the loss of their brother.

The Holy city was close, less than two miles away. The legalists have come to give comfort to those that Jesus truly loved in the death of their brother. There is not much we can say to those that have lost someone that they love to the great enemy, death.

I have not had the privilege of visiting Israel as yet, but I would guess that you could actually see Jerusalem from the town of Bethany, since it is on a mountain. The Holy city was in plain view, and yet death had come and snatched their brother from them. Jesus, the Master, had healed many, and raised people from the dead, and yet He had not showed up in time. How they must have grieved over a death they knew could have been prevented by the presence of the Christ.

When Martha heard that Jesus was coming, she went out to meet Him, but Mary stayed at home

Some are moving out to meet Jesus while others that love Him are still at home grieving in their hearts over the conditions of their brothers.

"Lord," Martha said to Jesus, "if you had been here my brother would not have died. But I know that even now God will give you whatever you ask."

The knowledge that Jesus overcame death on the cross and yet we are still subject to it is something that bothers all of us. We see our loved ones snatched from us, often in the prime of life. Martha knows God could reach down and eliminate this scourge from the earth, and she acknowledges the power of God over death.

Jesus said to her, "Your brother will rise again."

The Church will rise again; all that have gone to sleep before us will also rise up before us. The dead will rise and then those that are living will be snatched up to meet Him in the air.

Martha answered, "I know he will rise again in the resurrection at the last day."

Martha was obviously looking to the resurrection, saying what we all have said, "When, Lord, when will death be defeated?"

Jesus said to her, "I am the resurrection and the life. He who believes in Me will live, even though he dies: and whoever lives and believes in Me will never die. Do you believe this?"

We must believe that Jesus came to set us free from every curse of the enemy. The cross would defeat the enemy. When the Church finally believes this, and walks in the Power of it, He will come and rend the heavens to return for His beloved. Death is the last of the curses that will be put under our feet.

The disciples looked for Him over every hill they climbed for the rest of their lives. They searched the skies for signs and they waited with expectancy for their Lord to return. They wrapped each departed loved one with care and told them, "It's all right, He said He was coming soon." The years and the centuries have passed and with each one the hope of resurrection grew dimmer until a little over 100 years ago.

The Rapture was revealed from the Scriptures and people started looking again.

"Yes, Lord," she told Him, "I believe that you are the Christ, the Son of God, who was to come into the world."

So many believe that Jesus was the Christ that was to come, and that He did come, but they cannot see past the teachings of the organized Church to believe for the miracles. Christ did not come to leave us the same. He came for a radical change in the people that believed on Him. He came to be the miracle worker.

*And after she had said this, she went back
and called her sister Mary aside. "The
Teacher is here," she said, "and is asking
for you."*

Jesus is coming to teach us again. We have had
an avalanche of faith material released in this
generation. New methods of reviewing the
Scriptures and new evidence of God's hand from
the Bible code is pouring out upon the believer.
Jesus is asking for us to take a new look at the
traditions we have been taught.

*When Mary heard this, she got up quickly
and went to Him. Now Jesus was still at
the place where Martha had met Him.*

Martha the server was there and now Mary the
lover came quickly. Jesus is still waiting at the
place we need to go to receive revelation knowledge.

*When the Jews who had been with Mary in
the house, comforting her, noticed how
quickly she got up and went out, they
followed her, supposing she was going to
the tomb to mourn there.*

The legalists, represented by the Jews are there
with Mary, trying to comfort her. When she hears
Jesus is near she gets up and goes to Him.

The Jews follow her, thinking she is going to mourn at the tomb of the dead, rather than run to the giver of life. The worshipers and true followers of Christ are going to hear that He is showing up in congregations around the country, and they will run to Him. The legalists will follow and be there to witness the miracles.

When Mary reached the place where Jesus was and saw Him, she fell at His feet and said, "Lord, if you had been here, my brother would not have died."

As soon as Mary reached Jesus she fell at His feet. She knows that if He had been here there would have been no death.

When Jesus saw her weeping, and the Jews who had come along with her also weeping, He was deeply moved in spirit and troubled.

When His people weep, Jesus cares. He is moved in His Spirit, and grieved at our losses.

"Where have you laid him?" He asked. "Come and see, Lord," they replied.

He is searching for the Body that is His. He is weeping over the state of His beloved church. He will come and see; He will come and rescue us.

Jesus wept.

His tears are flowing for His beloved. The tears of Jesus are being shed for each one that is torn by grief, each one that is lost in death.

Then the Jews said, "See how much He loved him!"

There will be no doubt during the coming revival about how much God loves His people. In Malachi 3:18 the God writes, "And you will again see the distinction between the righteous and the wicked, between those who serve God and those who do not." God is going to pour blessings upon His people and there will be a line drawn between those that serve Him and those that serve satan.

It seems as though that line is already forming. I see those out of church fellowship increasingly coming under the influence of demons. There are studies that are coming out in the secular papers declaring that those who attend church regularly are healthier and live longer.

But some of them said, "Could not He who opened the eyes of the blind man have kept this man from dying?"

He is opening the blind eyes of the Church and He will indeed keep that Church from dying. There is going to be a great restoration to God's people of the power and glory He intended for His Church.

Jesus, once more deeply moved, came to the tomb. It was a cave with a stone laid across the entrance. "Take away the stone," He said.

The covering of the tomb is about to be moved away. A cave is tomb or a place to hide in the Scriptures. David hid in the cave of Adullam where he thirsted for water from the well at Bethlehem. The dead Church is unable to partake of the living water. Jesus is removing the barrier that separates Him from His Church.

"But Lord, said Martha, the sister of the dead man, "by this time there is a bad odor, for he has been there four days.

The dead Church stinks. It is lifeless and useless to battle against the powers of the air. It has lain there since the Church of acts, through the Catholic movement, into the reformation, and now in the renewal of the last 100 years, and it is dead.

Then Jesus said, "Did I not tell you that if you believed, you would see the glory of God?"

If we hold on to our faith in the Word of God, and believe in Him, Jesus is coming to wake up this corpse. We shall indeed see the glory of God fall upon the Church for this final hour of victory.

So they took away the stone. Then Jesus looked up and said, "Father, I thank you that you have heard Me. I knew that You always hear Me, but I said this for the benefit of the people standing here, that they may believe that you sent Me."

As the barrier between the dead Church and Jesus is removed, the people will finally believe in the complete victory of Christ over the rulers of darkness. We will defeat every demon, we will conquer every disease, we will win over poverty and lack, and then we will defeat death through the blood of Christ and the power of His name.

When He had said this, Jesus called in a loud voice, "Lazarus, come out!"

Jesus is shouting at us to come out of the tomb, leave the place of death and decay, and come to Him.

The dead man came out, his hands and feet wrapped with strips of linen, and a cloth around his face.

224

And the Church will come, bound with the grave cloths and with her face wrapped in the linen.

Jesus said to them, "Take off the grave clothes and let him go."

Those that have been freed will then set their brothers free. The Church shall no longer be bound by unbelief, but we shall function in total victory during this last day.

From Glory unto Glory

We recently had the privilege of sitting in a meeting led by Maurice Sklar. He spoke a message on the Last Days Church that was awesome. I had been feeling in my spirit that there was a prophetic word in the Transfiguration, and that Sunday afternoon between services I sat down to study it and the following revelation came to me.

I began to write about each line just as I did writing on the miracles, but in the middle of the first scripture, God began to speak to me directly. I am transcribing it exactly like He gave it to me.

Mark 9:2: "After 6 days Jesus took Peter, James and John with Him and led them up to a high mountain where they were all alone."

Six days represents the end of the Church age and places this right before the rapture of the Church. Peter, James and John are the inner circle, those that Jesus has taken into His heart and has revealed Himself to went up with Him. They are the leaders of the disciples. All of the others were left on the foot of the mountain.

The Lord says: "All of the believers will not be here for the Church of My Glory for many have died and many are not true followers of Me. My true followers will climb the mountain with Me."

Mark 9:3: "There He was transfigured before them. His clothes became dazzling white, whiter than anyone in this world could bleach them."

The Lord says: "I will take those that climb My mountain to a new level. The anointing of My glory will descend upon them and they will be clothed in the anointing of My presence. This will be a special heavenly anointing that cannot be achieved in this world, but must come from heaven. It is the Father's anointing."

Mark 9:4, "And there appeared before them Elijah and Moses, who were talking with Jesus."

The Lord says: "Elijah represents My prophets and Moses represents the Law. In this last hour of this last day My Word will become one and the fire of Elijah shall meet the righteousness of My Law in those that walk and talk with Me."

Mark 9:5. "Peter said to Jesus, "Rabbi, it is good for us to be here. Let us put up 3 shelters, one for You, one for Moses and one for Elijah." (He did not know what to say, they were so frightened.)

Other Books Available
By Lighthouse Publications

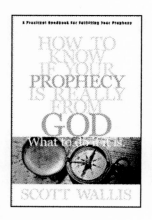 

These and other Christian books from
Lighthouse Publications are available at
participating local Christian bookstores,
Amazon.com & Bn.com.

Printed in the United States
1188200002B/214-312